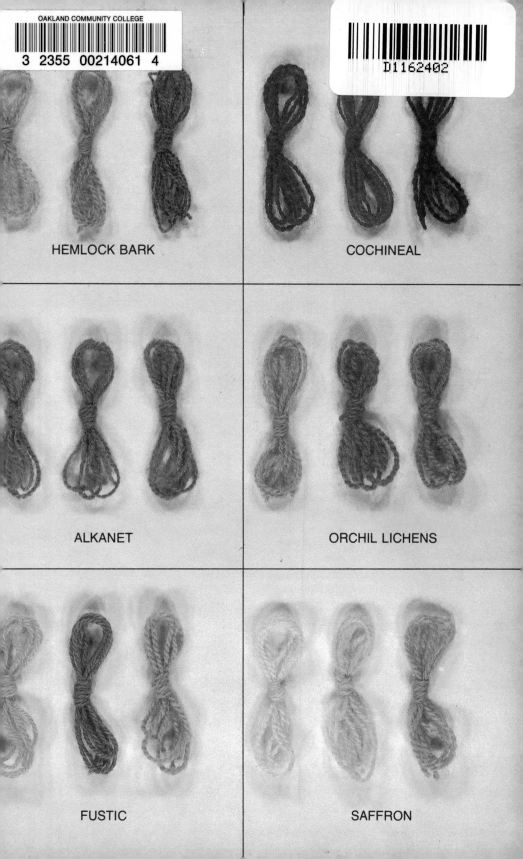

HEMLOCK BARK

COCHINEAL

ALKANET

ORCHIL LICHENS

FUSTIC

SAFFRON

# ANCIENT DYES FOR MODERN WEAVERS

BY PALMY WEIGLE

WATSON-GUPTILL PUBLICATIONS, NEW YORK

Library of Congress Cataloging in Publication Data
Weigle, Palmy, 1920-
    Ancient dye for modern weavers
    Bibliography: p.
    1. Dyes and dyeing, Domestic. 2. Dye plants.
I. Title.
TP909.W44        667'.3        74-6342
ISBN 0-8230-0223-3

First Printing, 1974

*To Betty, for her inspiration and encouragement*

# Contents

## 3. REDS, PURPLES, BLUES

## 4. YELLOWS, GOLDS, ORANGES

## 5. BROWNS, BLACKS

## 6. OVERDYEING

# *Introduction*

Love of color and the desire to surround oneself with it is not confined to the modern world. The Phoenicians, the Greeks, the Romans, and the inhabitants of ancient Peru all strove to find new sources of color. They looked to nature—plants, soil, rocks, and animals—to find useful things from which they could make their colors. By 3000 B.C. dyeing was a well-developed art in Mesopotamia, India, and Egypt. Early textile fragments, historical documents, and archeological artifacts give evidence of the skill with which the dyes of antiquity were used.

Today a new appreciation of "natural" color has developed. It stems in part from an increased interest in the environment and in part from many people's rejection of anything that is not "natural." It is not surprising, therefore, to find the artist-craftsman insisting on using natural dyes, and to find also that supply houses are now able to make the materials needed available. Madder, fustic, weld, alkanet—just the sound of these names conjures up the romance of the past. The purpose of this book is not only to explore the history and characteristics of these ancient dyes, but to give specific recipes for producing their many and varied colors.

# 1.
# Mordanting

# *Mordanting*

Some natural dyes have a make-up that does not permit them to unite readily with animal fibers—wool or alpaca for example. However, if another chemical is introduced then a bond can be created between the dyestuff and the fiber. These chemicals are called "mordants," a word that comes from the Latin word *mordere,* which means "to bite." It was thought that the mordant bit into the structure of the fiber, thus permitting the dye to enter. Actually this is not far removed from what does happen. The mordant acts on the molecules of the fibers, dissolving existing chemical links and forming new ones. These new molecules are then capable of uniting with dyestuffs that would normally be rejected by the fiber.

## Precautions

Any chemical can be dangerous to work with, and the same precautions that are recommended for other chemicals are also recommended for mordants:

1. Mordanting and dyeing should always be done in a well-ventilated room to help dispel any fumes.

2. Use rubber gloves as a protection for your hands and a smock or apron for your clothes.

3. Always add chemicals to water instead of water to chemicals (there will be less danger of adverse chemical reaction).

4. Above all, store mordants in a safe place—out of the reach of children or other inexperienced individuals.

### Mordants for Natural Dyes

The list that follows will provide a basic guide to both the characteristics and uses of the various mordants necessary in natural dyeing. Some mordants not only change the chemical composition of the dye, but can alter the colors that result and change the quality of the yarn.

*Alum (aluminum potassium sulfate).* A white mineral deposit that is a component of many types of rocks found in various parts of the world. (Aluminum potassium sulfate should not be confused with the aluminum ammonium sulfate, also called alum, found in grocery or drug stores, which will not give you satisfactory results.) Aluminum potassium sulfate was used as a mordant by the Romans and was documented by Pliny in his *Natural History.* The Indians of the Southwestern United States also have a long history of using a native alum found as a deposit where water evaporation has taken place around aluminum-bearing rocks. If too much aluminum potassium sulfate is used as a mordant, the yarn tends to be sticky. To help offset this possibility, alum is usually combined with cream of tartar.

*Cream of Tartar (potassium bitartrate).* A white powder that can be found in grocery stores among the baking supplies. It is formed during the fermentation process when making wine. In ancient times it was obtained by scraping the bottoms and sides of the wine casks. Cream of tartar is used with alum and sometimes with tin to help maintain the softness of woolen fibers.

*Chrome (potassium dichromate).* A bright orange crystalline substance that is very sensitive to light. For this reason it should be stored in a dark place and kept covered except when you are actually measuring out the amount needed. Chrome imparts a slight orange-tan color to the yarn in the mordanting process and is especially useful in dyeing golden or warm brown colors.

*Tin (stannous chloride).* White crystals that are light-sensitive, but to a lesser degree than chrome. Tin is found in Malaya, in Bolivia, where it has been mined since 1100 A.D., and in Cornwall, England, where the ancient Romans mined it successfully. Examining a copper-bronze alloy found in artifacts has enabled historians to trace tin back as far as 3500 B.C. Care must be exercised in using tin as a mordant because it has a tendency to make wool brittle. For this reason it is preferable to use tin as an additive to the dyebath instead of mordanting the yarn first. Its main function, which is to brighten a color, can be achieved by first dyeing the yarn, next adding tin to the dyebath, and then dyeing the yarn for a bit longer. This procedure reduces the length of time the tin will act on the yarn.

*Iron (ferrous sulfate).* A light green crystalline substance that is also called *green vitriol* or *copperas*. Iron ore was successfully smelted to make tools and containers in Asia Minor about 2000 B.C. Iron as a mordant is called a "saddening" agent because its main use is to deepen or darken a color. Too much exposure to iron can leave wool harsh and rough, so it is preferable to use it as an additive to the dyebath in the same manner as tin.

*Copper Sulfate (blue vitriol).* A bright blue substance that can be purchased as crystals or as a powder. The powder is preferable for dyeing because it dissolves far more readily than the crystals. Copper ore was used by early civilizations in Mesopotamia and India for producing many of their utensils. Copper sulfate used as a mordant will give yarn a slight bluish color. Treating copper with ammonia will provide a greenish blue dye, similar to the dye of the Chilkat Indians of the Pacific Northwest made by treating copper ore with urine. One of the main uses of copper sulfate is as an additive to change a yellow or a yellow-green to a definite green. It can also be used with some dyes to sadden the color.

*Tannin (tannic acid).* A light brown powder when purchased, it is found naturally in nuts, tree bark, and sumac plants. Gall nuts on oak trees were used as a mordant in antiquity. Dyestuff that already contains tannic acid (tea, for example) will not need a separate mordant, although color variations may be obtained by adding other mordants.

*Vinegar.* Vinegar is used as a mordant for its acetic acid content, especially in red dyebaths. White vinegar is preferable, and it can be used with the dyestuff in preparing the bath or added to the bath during dyeing. When used as an additive to a violet or purple dye, it will change the yarn to a reddish color.

*Baking Soda (bicarbonate of soda).* An alkali that is readily available in grocery or drug stores. As an additive it can change a violet or purple dye to a bluish color.

*Oxalic Acid.* A white powder that is generally used as an additive to increase the strength or restore the dye potential of a red dyebath.

*Ammonia (ammonium hydroxide).* Clear non-sudsy, non-detergent ammonia is the best type to use and may be found in grocery and hardware stores. It is especially useful in drawing the color out of grasses and lichens and may also be used to sharpen yellow or green dyebaths.

## Recipes for Mordanting

To aid the beginning dyer, the following recipes will use 1 ounce of wool and the amount of the chemical needed will be given in teaspoon measurements. The amounts work best on a two-ply medium-weight yarn. If a thinner or softer yarn is used, the amount of the mordant used should be reduced by 10 to 20 percent.

## Alum

1 ounce wool

1 quart water

1 teaspoon alum (loose)

1/2 teaspoon cream of tartar (loose)

In measuring the alum and the cream of tartar, do not pack them firmly in the spoon. It is preferable to have slightly less than to have extra. Dissolve the alum and cream of tartar in 1/4 cup warm water and add this to the quart of water, stirring to distribute the mordants evenly. Place the wet wool in the mordant bath and slowly bring the bath to a simmer over medium heat. This should take from 45 to 60 minutes. To keep the bath from getting hot too soon, either lower the heat or place an asbestos pad between the heat and the pan. The yarn may be moved around gently in the bath but do not stir it too much.

When the yarn has reached about 190°F. (tiny bubbles will start to appear around the rim of the pan), reduce the heat slightly and simmer the yarn for an additional 45 minutes. The yarn may be left to cool in the bath or it may be dyed immediately after squeezing out the excess moisture. Yarn to be kept for future dyeing may either be wrapped in a towel and stored in the refrigerator, or dried and then stored in a closet for future use.

## Chrome

1 ounce wool

1 quart water

1/16 teaspoon chrome

Dissolve 1/16 teaspoon chrome in 1/4 cup warm water and add this to 1 quart water, stirring to assure even distribution. Place the wet wool in the mordant bath, cover it, and bring it slowly to a simmer over medium heat (about 45 minutes). To keep the bath from heating too quickly, it may be necessary to lower the heat or to put an asbestos pad between the pan and the heat. It is essential that the cover be kept on during mordanting for proper results. The yarn may be moved around gently in the dyebath two or three times, but be sure to replace the cover on the pan.

When the bath has reached the simmering point, lower the heat and continue simmering for an additional 45 minutes. The yarn can be left to cool in the bath or dyed immediately after squeezing out the excess moisture. If the yarn will not be used right away, it should be wrapped in a towel, put in a plastic bag, and stored in a cool place such as the refrigerator. To avoid uneven color, the yarn should not be exposed to light before dyeing. Properly stored, chrome-mordanted yarn may be kept for 3 or 4 weeks before using.

## Tin

1/16 teaspoon stannous chloride (tin)

1 ounce wool

1 quart of dyebath

Dye 1 ounce of wool in 1 quart of dye that has been prepared according to the directions for the specific dye material. Remove the yarn from the dyebath and set it aside. Dissolve 1/16 teaspoon tin in 1/4 cup of warm water and add this to the dyebath, stirring to distribute it evenly. Put the dyed yarn back in the bath and simmer for an additional 15 minutes. Remove the yarn from the bath and rinse in mild soapy water. Rinse several more times without soap until the water is clear and free of color. The addition of tin will have the effect of brightening the color of the original dye.

## Iron

1/16 teaspoon ferrous sulfate

1 ounce of wool

1 quart of dyebath

Dye 1 ounce of wool in 1 quart of dye that has been prepared according to the directions for the specific dye material. Remove the yarn from the dyebath and set it aside. Dissolve completely 1/16 teaspoon iron in 1/4 cup of warm water and add this to the dyebath, stirring to distribute it evenly. Replace the dyed yarn in the bath and simmer for 15 minutes. Remove the yarn and rinse in mild soapy water. Rinse several more times without soap until the water is clear and free of color. Simmering the yarn in the dyebath with iron added will deepen or darken the original dye color because iron is a "saddening" agent.

## Copper Sulfate

1/2 teaspoon copper sulfate

1 ounce wool

1 quart of dyebath

Dye 1 ounce of wool in 1 quart of dye that has been prepared according to the directions for the specific dye material. Remove the yarn from the dyebath and set it aside. Dissolve 1/2 teaspoon copper sulfate in 1/4 cup of warm water and add this to the dyebath, stirring to distribute it evenly. Replace the dyed yarn in the bath and simmer for 15 minutes. Remove the yarn and rinse thoroughly. If the original dye was yellow or yellowish green, the color will become a true green. If a lighter green is desired, the amount of copper sulfate should be reduced to 1/4 teaspoon per quart of dye. If a deeper green is desired, the amount of copper sulfate can be increased to 3/4 teaspoon per quart of dyebath without damaging the quality of the yarn.

# 2.
# Dyeing

# Dyeing

This chapter will explore the equipment and procedures involved in natural dyeing, as well as give information about labeling yarn, recording dyeing results, and testing yarn for color fastness. Frequently, natural dyes are incorrectly contrasted with chemical dyes. All dyes have a chemical make-up, just as all fibers have a chemical composition. There are dyes that are made from materials found in nature such as roots, fruit, or leaves—these are natural dyes. Then there are dyes made in laboratories from combining purified or isolated components—these are synthetic dyes.

## Equipment

Because chemicals do have an effect on yarn, it is important to use pans that will not change the nature of the yarn during the mordanting and dyeing process. The best pans to use are those made of enamel or stainless steel. Care should be taken to avoid chipping the inside of the enamel pans because the exposed metal underneath may leak into the dyebath and darken the yarn. Should chips develop, many hardware stores carry tubes of liquid enamel for repairing the chipped areas. Any pan used should be large enough to accommodate the yarn and the liquid dye with a little room to spare. A pan that is 1/2 to 1 quart larger than the amount of dyebath gives some extra room for stirring the bath and at the same time is not so large that the liquid will not cover the yarn completely.

Copper and brass pans have a tendency to brighten the colors produced while iron pans will darken them. Aluminum pans will also brighten colors, but some mordants will cause pitting on the inner surface.

Stainless steel, enamel, or wooden spoons should be used for stirring the dyebath. Do not use darkly stained wooden spoons in a light dyebath, however, or the stain might affect the color produced. In dyeing small amounts of yarn, wooden chopsticks make very useful stirrers. Other articles of equipment necessary for dyeing include the following:

1. A small postal scale to weigh small amounts of yarn or dyestuffs.

2. A glass measuring cup that has a 1 or 2 cup capacity.

3. A large strainer.

4. Plastic pans or pails for rinsing yarn.

5. Stainless steel or plastic measuring spoons for measuring mordants.

6. Cheesecloth in which to tie dyestuffs.

7. Asbestos pads to put under hot pans.

8. Rubber gloves (preferably lined).

9. A smock or apron to protect your clothes.

*Water.* Unless a recipe specifically states otherwise, soft water works best for dyeing. If your water will make soap suds readily without leaving scum, it is soft enough to use without adding a softener. If the water is too hard, add a small amount of one of the water softeners available in grocery or hardware stores (add only the minimum amount necessary to soften the water). Acetic acid or vinegar may also be used to neutralize hard water. If a recipe requires hard water, add a small amount of powdered chalk to the soft water (1/4 to 1/2 teaspoon chalk to 1 quart water).

## Preparing Yarn

When selecting wool yarn to use in natural dyeing, it is best to use a natural, unbleached yarn. Natural yarn is likely to turn the predicted color, whereas a bleached, whitened yarn is apt to turn out slightly different because of the effect of the chemicals used in bleaching. Fortunately there are now many suppliers providing natural yarns in a variety of weights.

The first step in preparing the yarn is to make skeins that are easy to handle. It will be helpful to decide on a standard weight for all the skeins to be used in the dyepots. Then you can always be sure that the proper amount of yarn is being used in any given amount of dye by counting the skeins. A minimum of a quart of dye is needed for each ounce of wool to be dyed. Each quart of dye is therefore able to accommodate an ounce of wool, or 2 skeins of yarn each weighing 1/2 ounce. This book uses 1/2 ounce skeins as a standard.

Various types and sizes of skein winders are available, but you can easily make skeins by bending your arm and winding the yarn around your elbow and hand. Make a few practice skeins to find out how many winds are necessary to produce the yarn weight desired. The reason for using 1/2 ounce skeins in this book is for ease of handling, plus the belief that most dyers would prefer to try out new recipes in small amounts.

After the wool is wound into skeins, the ends of the yarn should be tied together in a knot. Then tie the skeins loosely in several places in a figure eight, using mercerized white cotton string. For 1/2 ounce skeins, 3 such ties should be sufficient to keep the skeins from becoming tangled during dyeing. Be sure not to tie the string too tightly around the skein or the dye may not penetrate the tied areas sufficiently.

After the skeins are tied, they should be washed in lukewarm water with a mild soap or a very mild detergent. Rinse them thoroughly and squeeze out the excess moisture. Do not wring or twist skeins of yarn.

## Preparing Fleece

Fleece that is dyed before it is spun is called "dyed-in-the-wool." If you prefer to dye fleece, first be sure to remove the foreign matter and dirt. Badly soiled or stained areas should be discarded because they tend not to accept the dye. The fleece should then soak in warm water and mild soap or detergent. Do not use strong soap or detergent, however, or too much natural lanolin will be removed from the fleece and will make it more difficult to spin. When the fleece has soaked for several hours, rinse it gently in warm water. Allow the water to drain out of the fleece and then leave it to dry. Avoid excess handling or the fleece may mat.

When mordanting or dyeing fleece, it can be loosely tied in cheesecloth (or a similar open-weave fabric). It should be pointed out that various parts of the same fleece may take the dye differently. Proper sorting and carding before spinning will help achieve a more uniform color. You can obtain interesting effects by dyeing fleece separately in dyebaths of different colors. The fleece may then be carded and spun together to produce a heather effect in the yarn.

## Collection and Storage of Dyestuffs

Although many of the dye materials needed for the recipes in this book will have to be ordered from supply houses, there are a few basic guidelines that the beginning dyer will want to follow in the collection and storage of natural dyestuffs.

The basic rule is to gather the dye material when the part of the plant you want to use is at its strongest stage of development. Flowers should be picked just as they are reaching their peak of blooming. Berries should be gathered when they are completely ripe and full of juice. In most cases, leaves should be taken in late spring when they are fully developed. Bark will give best color when it comes from mature trees. Although bark may be taken from live trees in small amounts without killing the trees, your local nursery may be able to provide you with bark from trees already cut down. Avoid gathering those plants that are on conservation lists. Do not strip the landscape; make it a rule to leave at least as much as you have gathered.

While it is true that the dyebath will generally be stronger if fresh plant material is used, many plants may be dried or frozen for future use with success. To preserve flowers, roots, bark, and leaves, air-dry them on wiremesh set up so air can circulate freely all around it. The dried material should then be placed in paper bags and kept in a dry place.

Berries can be dried, but the color produced is better if they are quick-frozen while still fresh. Wash the berries well, drain them, and pack them in plastic bags or containers. Make a note of the amount in each container so you do not have to defrost them before using. Always label the packages very carefully before freezing so these packages are not mistaken for food. Some berries (such as pokeberries) are poisonous and should not be stored where young children can get at them.

## Dyeing the Yarn

After the yarn has been washed and mordanted (if necessary), it is ready to be dyed. The skeins should always be wet before they are placed in a dyebath to help guarantee an even dye. If dry skeins are put in a dyebath, the parts of the skein that first come in contact with the dye immediately begin to absorb the dye and when fully dyed will have a deeper color than the rest of the skein.

Woolen yarn should not be subjected to abrupt changes in temperature. If the yarn is to be placed in a warm dyebath, it should first be gradually raised to the temperature of the dyebath. To do this, put the yarn in a pan with cool water and slowly add some hot water. The warm yarn can then be placed in a warm dyebath without causing it to tighten up and lose its softness. The dyebath should never be allowed to boil when there is yarn in it. Some recipes will give specific optimum temperatures, but the general rule is not to exceed 190°F. whenever there is yarn in the dyebath (the boiling point of water is 212°F.).

When the dyebath reaches the simmering point, start timing it according to the directions of the recipe. While it is simmering, move the skeins around gently so all the yarn is dyed evenly. To keep the bath from becoming too hot, it may be necessary to turn the heat down or off for a while. Asbestos pads may also be placed between the pan and the heat to reduce the temperature. At the end of the specified time the dyed yarn is ready to be removed from the bath.

If you want a lighter color than produced in the recipe, simmer the yarn for a shorter time. Another method is to use the same dyebath two or three times (lighter colors will be produced each time). If a darker color is desired, allow the yarn to simmer for a longer time or leave it to cool in the dyebath overnight. Always bear in mind that the color of wet yarn is darker than the color will be when the yarn is rinsed and dried.

## Several Colors from One Dyebath

It is possible to obtain several colors simultaneously from one dyebath by placing unmordanted skeins, alum-mordanted skeins, and chrome-mordanted skeins in the dyebath together. In following this procedure for a number of years now, I have not found that the mordants noticeably affect each other.

To be sure which mordants have been applied to which skeins, identifying buttons of clear glass can be attached to the skeins (glass will not absorb dye). For example, round buttons could designate alum-mordanted skeins and diamond-shaped ones could signify chrome-mordanted skeins. No button attached would mean that no mordant was used. Attach the buttons by small loops of string to the twine tied around the skein.

If this system is followed, there should be no doubt as to which mordants produced the different effects on the dyed yarn. When doing test baths to explore the possible range of color from one dyebath, the yarn should always be labeled carefully before the buttons are removed. If the string on the button takes on any of the dye, it should be replaced with clean string before the buttons are reused.

## Rinsing and Drying Yarn

After the yarn is dyed, it should be rinsed thoroughly until the rinse water becomes clear. The temperature of the first rinse should be approximately the same as the dyebath at the time the yarn is taken out. Successive rinses can be gradually reduced in temperature. If the yarn is removed from a hot dyebath, the first rinse bath would be hot. If, on the other hand, the yarn is allowed to cool in the dyebath, a cool rinse would be used. When auxiliary mordants such as tin and iron are used, the first rinse should contain some mild soap or detergent. If the yarn seems a little hard or stiff, 1/3 cup of vinegar per quart of water will help make it softer.

Continue rinsing the yarn until all the excess dye has been removed and the water stays clear. The removal of the unabsorbed dye will help to prevent the color from "bleeding" out of the yarn later on. "Guaranteed to bleed" fabrics are easy to produce by failing to remove excess dye!

The yarn should then be gently squeezed to remove as much moisture as possible. Label the skeins as outlined in the following section and let them dry out of the direct sunlight. Drying can be hastened by rolling the yarn in a towel, then laying it flat on another, dry, towel during the drying. If the skeins are hung up to dry, they should be turned or rotated occasionally to hasten the drying and to help keep the dye from collecting at the bottom.

## Labeling

Small tags—such as those used for labels on merchandise—may be purchased at a stationery store for use in identifying the dyed skeins. The labels should be attached to the skeins as soon as they come out of the bath while the pertinent information is still fresh in your mind. The following information should be recorded on the labels:

1. Name of the dye material.

2. Name of the mordant (if any) used before dyeing.

3. Name of the mordant (if any) added to the dyebath.

4. Date of dyeing.

5. Any change from the recipe (for example simmering for a shorter time than specified).

Skeins so labeled can be a help in deciding what use to make of a particular dye material when planning projects.

## Keeping Records

Before dyed skeins are used in weaving or needlework projects, a permanent record should be made of each color. Use a large looseleaf notebook with unlined white paper. Clear acetate envelopes to enclose the sheets of paper are recommended but not essential.

Each dye material should have a separate sheet. At the top of the sheet write the name of the dyestuff (for example madder). On that sheet keep a record of each color resulting from that particular dyestuff. Attach several 2" strands of each color produced down the right-hand side of the page. A small stapler is the easiest way to attach them. Opposite each variation of color, write the name of the mordant or mordants used and any other pertinent information. The sheet for madder might look like this:

---

## MADDER

| Premordant | Additive | Yarn Samples |
|---|---|---|
| Alum | None | ———————— |
| Alum | Tin | ———————— |
| Chorme | None | ———————— |
| Chrome | Iron | ———————— |
| None | None | ———————— |

---

When a subsequent dyebath produces a noticeable difference in color, a record of the change should be made. Be sure to note what caused the difference, if you can tell. Complete records will be especially helpful when you are planning a new weaving project. If you need several variations of a color, you can refer to your notebook to determine which dye material can give you the desired range of colors.

## Testing for Color Fastness

The question most frequently asked about natural dyes is, "Are they fast colors?" The answer lies in the realization that the first synthetic dye was made in 1856. A visit to any of the fine textile museums will furnish the opportunity to see firsthand the range and clarity in many of the fabrics and tapestries from the time of the ancient Egyptians or Peruvians through the present day.

The primary concern today is for colors that are fast to sunlight, since fabrics that are not fast to washing may be dry-cleaned. To test for color fastness to sunlight, samples of the dyed yarns should be attached to a board (or strong cardboard) with the names of the dyes and mordants listed opposite each color. Write the date the test is started on the board. Then cover half of every sample with a strip of black plastic so the sun will act only on the uncovered yarn. Place the samples in a sunny window, preferably with a southern exposure, for maximum sunlight. The test may be made outdoors if you live in an area where highway, factory, or airway pollution is not a factor.

If the test for fastness is made outdoors, 12 days of exposure in summer is sufficient; if the test is made in winter or late fall, add four or five days more to make up for the shorter daylight hours. For a test made indoors in a sunny exposure allow a full four weeks.

At the end of that time, remove the covering and compare the two halves of each sample. If the color has faded to a much lighter shade, that dye should be classified as a fugitive dye. If the color is still basically the same color but not as strong, it may be considered a medium-fast color that could be used where it would not have continuous exposure to sunlight. If the color is unchanged or almost as strong as when the test began, that dye would be considered a very fast dye.

It is advisable for anyone who wishes to use naturally dyed yarns in weaving or needlework to do a color fastness test. Although some recipes may state that a dye is color fast, it is best to assure yourself that you are achieving the same degree of success in your own dyeing before beginning a major project.

# 3.
# Reds
# Purples
# Blues

# Madder
## RED

Madder (*Rubia tinctorum*) is one of the most ancient dyes, and its color fastness ranks among the best. In ancient times the Egyptians used madder as a dye, as did the early Hebrews. Herodotus, the Greek historian, described its use as a dye for clothing in Libya. Pliny the Elder wrote that madder was grown near Rome during the first century A.D. It eventually became a major item of trade between the Orient and Europe. By the Middle Ages, Holland, France, and Italy were growing madder in sufficient quantity to supply many of the cloth merchants of Europe. It is interesting to note that madder was known to the Florentines as "rubia," the origin of the name of the famous della Robbia family.

The source of the dye is the red material beneath the outer bark of the roots of the madder plant. The plant should be three years old before the roots are large enough to be used profitably. In rich soil they may reach a length of two feet or more, but they are only one quarter inch in diameter. In early fall, the roots are dug up, washed, and then dried in the air or in kilns. Before they are used, the roots are normally powdered in order to release the color more readily in the dyebath.

Madder can be purchased from dye supply houses, either in the form of small pieces of chopped roots or as a powder. The pieces of root should be pulverized by wrapping them in a small muslin bag, laying this on a hard surface, then pounding with a hammer. A blender or food grinder can also be used for this purpose, but if you use these appliances for this purpose, do *not* use them for food too. In addition, the blender or grinder should be cleaned meticulously after each use to be sure that there is no carryover when another dye material is pulverized.

In the dyeing process, bear in mind that too much heat for a prolonged time can alter the intensity of the red or change it to a brownish tone. For this reason, it is preferable to soak the roots or powder in water overnight before preparing the dyebath.

## Preparing the Dyebath

1 ounce madder roots

2 quarts water

Tie the chopped or powdered roots in a small cheesecloth bag and soak the bag in 2 quarts of water for about 12 hours (or overnight). After the roots have soaked, heat them for an hour in the same water over low or medium heat, and gradually bring the bath to the boiling point. Let the dyebath boil for 10 minutes and then immediately remove the pan from the heat. Remove the cheesecloth bag and the roots from the bath, then add enough water to make 2 quarts of dye. Divide this liquid into 2 equal parts to use as dye for the following recipes.

## 1. Madder with Alum (Red)

1 quart dyebath

2 skeins of alum-mordanted wool (1/2 ounce each)

Using half of the 2 quarts of dye you have made, place 2 wet skeins of alum-mordanted yarn in the dyebath and simmer for 30 minutes. Remove the yarn, and rinse and label one skein. The yarn will be a strong red. Set the other skein aside to use in the next recipe.

## 2. Madder with Alum plus Tin (Orange-Red)

1 quart dyebath

1 skein alum-mordanted wool (1/2 ounce)

1/16 teaspoon stannous chloride (tin)

Use the same bath as in Recipe 1 (it will now be slightly less than a quart). Dissolve 1/16 teaspoon of stannous chloride in 1/4 cup of water. Add this to the madder bath and stir to distribute the tin evenly in the bath. Place the second skein of yarn—already alum-mordanted for Recipe 1—back in the bath and simmer gently for 15 minutes. Remove the skein and rinse, first in soapy water and then in clear water. The yarn will be an orange-red, brighter than the skein from Recipe 1 because tin is a brightening agent.

### 3. Madder with Chrome (Garnet)

1 quart dyebath
2 skeins chrome-mordanted wool (1/2 ounce each)

Using the second quart of madder dye from Recipe 1 as a base, place 2 wet skeins of chrome-mordanted yarn in the dyebath. Be sure that the pan you are using is small enough so the yarn is completely covered by the liquid. Simmer the yarn for 30 minutes, then remove both skeins. The yarn will be a garnet-red. Rinse and label one skein and set the other skein aside to use in the next recipe.

### 4. Madder with Chrome plus Iron (Dull Garnet)

1 quart dyebath
1 skein chrome-mordanted yarn (1/2 ounce)
1/16 teaspoon iron

Use the same bath as in Recipe 3. Dissolve 1/16 teaspoon iron in 1/4 cup hot water and add this to the madder bath. Stir thoroughly to distribute the iron evenly in the bath. Place the second skein of yarn—already mordanted and dyed in Recipe 3—in the madder-iron bath and simmer for 15 minutes. Remove the skein and rinse, first in soapy water and then in clear water. The yarn will be a garnet shade, darker than in Recipe 3 because iron is a saddening agent.

The above recipes show how four variations of color can be readily produced from one initial dyebath. Should you desire to make only one of the colors, prepare the dyebath in the same manner as before. For each ounce of wool to be dyed, 1/2 ounce of madder is used with 1 quart of water.

### 5. Madder with Alum (Red)

1 quart dyebath
2 skeins alum-mordanted wool (1/2 ounce each)

Place the wet alum-mordanted skeins in the dyebath and simmer gently for 30 minutes. Remove the skeins and rinse them thoroughly. The yarn will be a strong red.

## 6. Madder with Alum plus Tin (Orange-Red)

1 quart dyebath

2 skeins alum-mordanted wool (1/2 ounce each)

1/16 teaspoon stannous chloride (tin)

Place the 2 wet alum-mordanted skeins in the dyebath (*without* the tin). Simmer them for 30 minutes, then remove both skeins (now dyed red). Dissolve 1/16 teaspoon tin in 1/4 cup of water. Add this to the madder bath, stirring to evenly distribute the tin. Put both skeins back in the bath and simmer gently for 15 minutes. Remove both skeins and rinse them, first in soapy water and then in clear water. The yarn has changed in color from red to orange-red.

Tin should not be added to the dyebath initially because it has a tendency to make wool brittle. By dyeing the skeins first and then adding the tin to change the red to orange-red, the wool is exposed to the effects of tin for a shorter length of time.

## 7. Madder with Chrome (Garnet)

1 quart dyebath

2 skeins chrome-mordanted wool (1/2 ounce each)

Place the 2 wet skeins of chrome-mordanted yarn in the dyebath and simmer them gently for 30 minutes. Remove the skeins and rinse them well. The yarn will be a garnet-red.

## 8. Madder with Chrome plus Iron (Dull Garnet)

1 quart dyebath

2 skeins chrome-mordanted wool (1/2 ounce each)

1/16 teaspoon iron

Place the 2 wet skeins of chrome-mordanted yarn in the dyebath and simmer gently for 30 minutes. Remove the skeins, now dyed a garnet-red. Dissolve 1/16 teaspoon iron in 1/4 cup of hot water. Add it to the dyebath, stirring to distribute it evenly. Place both skeins back in the dyebath and simmer for 15 minutes. Remove the skeins and rinse, first in soapy water and then in clear water. The skeins are now saddened to a darker garnet shade.

Iron should not be added to the dyebath initially because it has a tendency to make wool harsh. By dyeing the skeins garnet first and then adding iron to change the color to a dull garnet, the wool is exposed to the effects of iron for a shorter length of time.

# Pokeberry
## RED

Pokeweed (*Phytolacca americana*) is a perennial shrub native to many parts of the United States and Canada. In early spring the very young shoots can be used as a food if prepared properly, which accounts for pokeweed sometimes being called "American spinach." The plants, once established, can grow to a height of six to ten feet and produce many clusters of berries. In the late summer or early fall the berries turn a deep purple-black when they are ripe. Pokeberry dye was a favorite of the American Indians for staining their baskets.

The dyestuff is contained in these berries. They are a favored food of many birds, but it should be noted that they are poisonous to humans. The berries should be gathered when they are fully ripened and may be used fresh to produce a strong red color. If you cannot use them when they are fresh, they can be quick-frozen for later use. Freeze them in pint or quart containers and there will be no need to defrost them before they are used.

Crushing the berries and then soaking them overnight will help draw out the deep red juice. Pokeberries can also be allowed to ferment for a month, but the colors produced will be more purple than red. Care should be taken not to use too much heat with pokeberries or the color will change from a clear red to a rusty or a muddy brown.

The dye obtained from pokeberries is unfortunately not fast to sunlight. In doing a fastness test on pokeberry dye, you will find that in two weeks the color will lose some of its brilliance. After about six weeks of exposure to full sunlight, the color may fade to a weak pink. When kept out of direct sunlight, however, the color will last for several years.

## Preparing the Dyebath

2 quarts ripe pokeberries
1 quart water

Tie the 2 quarts of ripe pokeberries in a cheesecloth bag and put this in a pan with 1 quart of water. With a stainless steel or clean wooden spoon press down on the berries to crush them and release the juice. Leave the berries to soak overnight. This preparation of pokeberries will apply to Recipes 9 and 10.

## 9. Pokeberries with Vinegar (Red)

2 quarts pokeberries soaking in 1 quart of water
2 skeins of unmordanted wool (1/2 ounce each)
1 cup white vinegar
1 quart water

Mix 1/2 cup white vinegar in 1 quart of water. Place the wet unmordanted yarn in this solution and simmer for 45 minutes. Remove the skeins but do not rinse. Add the vinegar-water and the remaining 1/2 cup vinegar to the pokeberries and water. Simmer gently for 45 minutes, pressing down on the berries with a spoon to help release all the color. Do not boil or the color may be dulled. Remove the cheesecloth bag with the berries, squeezing it to get out all of the juice.

Place the wet vinegar-mordanted skeins of yarn in the dyebath and simmer for 45 minutes. Stir the bath gently from time to time to help assure an even color. The yarn may be left to cool in the dyebath, then removed and allowed to dry before rinsing. If it is laid flat on several sheets of paper towels, the excess dye will be absorbed evenly. Drying the yarn before rinsing permits the red color to become stronger. After 24 hours the yarn should be rinsed until the water is clear. The yarn will be a strong red. Alum-mordanted or chrome-mordanted yarn may be used, but they have a tendency to dull the color.

## 10. Pokeberries with Vinegar plus Oxalic Acid (Bright Red)

2 quarts pokeberries soaking in 1 quart of water
2 skeins of unmordanted wool (1/2 ounce each)
1 cup white vinegar
1/16 teaspoon oxalic acid

Mix 1/2 cup white vinegar in 1 quart of water. Place the wet unmordanted skeins of yarn in this solution and simmer for 45 minutes. Remove the skeins, but do not rinse. Add the vinegar-water and the remaining 1/2 cup of vinegar to the pokeberries and water. Simmer gently for 45 minutes, pressing down on the berries with a spoon to help release the color. Do not boil or the color may be dulled. Remove the cheesecloth bag with the berries, squeezing it to get out all the juice. Place the wet vinegar-treated skeins in the pokeberry and vinegar bath and simmer gently for 30 minutes. Remove the skeins and set them aside. Dissolve 1/16 teaspoon oxalic acid in 1/4 cup water and add to the dyebath, stirring to distribute it evenly. Return the skeins to the bath and simmer for an additional 15 minutes. Remove the skeins and let them dry for 24 hours before rinsing them until the water comes clear. The yarn will be a red color, brighter than that obtained in Recipe 9. Color fastness tests show that in 3 weeks the yarn has lost some of its brilliance, but it is still a medium-red color.

## 11. Pokeberries Fermented Naturally (Purple)

2 quarts ripe pokeberries
1 quart water
2 skeins unmordanted wool (1/2 ounce each)

Place the pokeberries and water in a pan. Cover the pan loosely so any gas formed during fermentation may escape easily. Keep the pan in a cool place (50° to 65°F.) for about 4 weeks. The liquid should now be a deep reddish purple color and will have a slight scum on the surface. Strain out the berries and the dyebath is ready to use. If necessary, add water to bring the bath up to a full quart.

Place the wet skeins of unmordanted yarn in the quart of dyebath and simmer over low heat for 45 minutes. Let the yarn cool in the dyebath and then let it dry without rinsing. After it is thoroughly dry, rinse it until the water is clear. The yarn will be purple instead of red, but it is not fast to sunlight. Alum-mordanted and chrome-mordanted skeins may be used but they will produce colors that are more brown than purple.

# *Hemlock Bark*

## ROSE TO GRAY

The hemlock (*Tsuga canadensis*), also called Eastern hemlock or spruce pine, was an important tree for the early people of North America. The twigs and leaves were used to make a medicinal tea and the bark boiled to furnish a thick paste to help heal wounds. This Eastern hemlock is quite different from the European hemlock (*Conium maculatum*) that provided the poisonous extract for Socrates to drink. In colonial days, brooms were made from the young branches of the hemlock. In the garden of the governor's palace in Williamsburg, Virginia, hemlock trees were used for ornamental hedges.

The bark of the hemlock is an important source of tannin (tannic acid) and dye. The Chilkat Indians used it to help produce the black colors of their twined blankets. Other Indian tribes used it for dyeing both basket materials and porcupine quills. Because it was rich in tannin, it was used for tanning leather. As a dye, hemlock bark can produce a range of colors from a rose-tan to a slate gray depending on the mordant used.

To gather bark, enlist the aid of a local nursery or a landscape gardener. If there are hemlock trees that need to be shaped, the bark from the branches will furnish good dye material. A sharp knife will easily strip away the dark outer bark with red-purple streaks inside. The bark may be used fresh or dried for future use.

## Preparing the Dyebath

1 ounce hemlock bark

1 quart water

Cut the bark into small strips or pieces and tie it in a cheesecloth bag. Put it in 1 quart of water to soak for 24 hours. After soaking, boil the bark and water vigorously for an hour, adding water occasionally if needed. If the bark is taken from older trees, it is advisable to boil it for at least a half-hour more. After boiling, remove the cheesecloth bag containing the bark. Add enough water to the bath to make 1 quart of dye. For each ounce of wool to be dyed in any of the following recipes, 1 quart of dyebath must be prepared.

## 12. Hemlock Bark on Unmordanted Yarn (Warm Beige)

1 quart dyebath

2 skeins unmordanted wool (1/2 ounce each)

Place the 2 wet skeins of unmordanted yarn in 1 quart of dyebath and simmer for 45 minutes. Remove the skeins and rinse thoroughly. The yarn will be a warm beige with a pink feeling to it.

## 13. Hemlock Bark with Alum (Rose-Tan)

1 quart dyebath

2 skeins alum-mordanted wool (1/2 ounce each)

Place the 2 wet skeins of alum-mordanted yarn in 1 quart of dyebath and simmer for 45 minutes. Remove the skeins and rinse thoroughly. The yarn will be a rose-tan color. The color will be deeper if the skeins are allowed to cool in the dyebath before rinsing.

## 14. Hemlock Bark with Chrome (Tan)

1 quart dyebath

2 skeins chrome-mordanted wool (1/2 ounce each)

Place the 2 wet skeins of chrome-mordanted yarn in 1 quart of dyebath and simmer for 45 minutes. Remove the skeins and rinse thoroughly. The color is a medium tan, but deeper than those resulting from the previous recipes. The color may be deepened further by allowing the skeins to cool in the dyebath before rinsing.

## 15. Hemlock Bark with Iron (Gray)

1 quart dyebath

2 skeins unmordanted wool (1/2 ounce each)

1/16 teaspoon iron

Place the 2 wet skeins of unmordanted yarn in 1 quart of dyebath and simmer for 30 minutes. Remove the skeins and set them aside. Dissolve 1/16 teaspoon iron in 1/4 cup water and add this to the dyebath, stirring to distribute it evenly. Replace the skeins in the bath and simmer gently for 15 minutes more. Remove the skeins and rinse, first in soapy water and then in clear water. The skeins are a warm gray color and may be deepened further by allowing the yarn to cool in the dyebath before rinsing.

Note: All of the dyebaths mentioned are still capable of dyeing additional skeins of yarn to produce lighter colors than those achieved with the first use.

# Cochineal
## RED

Cochineal is a red dye made from an insect (*Dactylopius coccus*) that was originally cultivated on cactus plants in Mexico, Central America, and the Canary Islands. Its dye potential was known and used by the Aztec Indians in Mexico long before the Spanish invasions of the early sixteenth century. The Spanish brought the dye to Europe, where it replaced kermes, the red dye obtained from the oak tree shield louse. Kermes dye had been used since antiquity and was mentioned in the writings of Moses.

Cochineal proved to be a superior dye to kermes and a more profitable one because it could be grown year round in warm climates. The insects grow from birth to maturity in three months. There are two types of cochineal dye: silver, produced from the impregnated females before they lay their eggs, and dark, produced from the females after the eggs are laid. Great care is taken to gather the cochineal as a silver crop because it produces a better color and can be sold for a greater price.

At the right time of year the insects are brushed off the leaves and stems of the cactus with soft brushes (sometimes squirrel tails are used instead of brushes). There are several methods of killing the insects: immersing them in scalding water, heating them in an oven for a few hours, drying them in the hot sun, or even agitating them back and forth in sacks (which incidentally helps give them a shiny appearance). In a good year three crops can be gathered at the rate of about 200 pounds per acre. It is said that one pound of dye powder contains 70,000 dried bugs. One pound of yarn may be dyed a deep red with two ounces of cochineal. The cochineal powder may be purchased from dye supply houses.

## Preparing the Dyebath

1/4 ounce cochineal

1 quart water

Tie 1/4 ounce cochineal powder in a cheesecloth bag and put it in 1 quart of water to soak for 3 or 4 hours, or overnight if that is more convenient. After soaking, bring the cochineal bath to the boiling point and boil it vigorously for 15 minutes. Remove the bath from the heat and take out the cheesecloth bag with the cochineal. Add enough water to make 1 quart of dyebath. For each ounce of yarn to be dyed according to any of the following recipes, 1 quart of dyebath must be prepared.

## 16. Cochineal with Alum (Crimson)

1 quart dyebath

2 skeins alum-mordanted wool (1/2 ounce each)

Place the 2 wet skeins of alum-mordanted yarn in 1 quart of dyebath. Simmer gently for 1 hour, and then allow the skeins to cool in the dyebath. After cooling, remove the skeins and rinse. The yarn will be a crimson red.

## 17. Cochineal with Tin and Cream of Tartar (Scarlet)

1 quart dyebath

2 skeins unmordanted wool (1/2 ounce each)

1/16 teaspoon tin

1/8 teaspoon cream of tartar

Place the 2 wet skeins of unmordanted yarn in 1 quart of dyebath and simmer gently for 45 minutes. Remove the skeins and set them aside. Dissolve 1/16 teaspoon tin and 1/8 teaspoon cream of tartar in 1/4 cup water and add it to the dyebath, stirring to distribute it evenly. Replace the skeins in the bath and simmer an additional 30 minutes. Allow the skeins to cool in the dyebath and then rinse, first in soapy water and then in clear water. The yarn will be a vibrant scarlet.

## 18. Cochineal with Chrome plus Vinegar (Purple)

1 quart dyebath

2 skeins chrome-mordanted wool (1/2 ounce each)

2 teaspoons white vinegar

Add 2 teaspoons white vinegar to 1 quart of dyebath. Place 2 wet skeins of chrome-mordanted yarn in the cochineal-vinegar dyebath and simmer gently for 1 hour. Allow the skeins to cool in the dyebath and then rinse thoroughly. The yarn will be a deep reddish purple.

## 19. Cochineal with Vinegar (Light Purple)

1 quart dyebath

2 skeins unmordanted wool (1/2 ounce each)

Place the 2 wet skeins of unmordanted yarn in 1 quart of dyebath and simmer gently for 1 hour. Allow the skeins to cool in the dyebath and then rinse thoroughly. The yarn will be a light purple.

Note: All of the dyebaths still have dyeing potential. They may be used to dye new skeins of yarn in less intense variations of the colors first produced. Another interesting way to use them is to add other mordants, such as 1/16 teaspoon iron or 1/4 teaspoon copper sulfate, to make gray or gray-purple. If 1/16 teaspoon oxalic acid is added to the cochineal bath without the vinegar, it will serve to renew the bath and produce redder colors.

# Sandalwood
## RED

Sandalwood (*Pterocarpus santalinus*), also called sanders wood or santal wood, is a tropical tree native to India, Ceylon, and the tropical areas of Asia. Although it has long been known as a dye, its use has not been extensive because the wood is extremely hard and is reluctant to give up its color.

The heartwood of the tree is the potential source of the dye. It is a fine-grained wood and has a strong brick-red color. To prepare it for sale as a dye, the wood is cut into blocks and then chipped into small pieces or ground to a powder. The range of reds obtainable is not easily duplicated by other dye materials. Sandalwood chips may be purchased from dye supply houses.

### Preparing the Dyebath

1 ounce sandalwood chips
1 quart water

Tie 1 ounce of sandalwood chips in a cheesecloth bag and put it in 1 quart of water to soak for at least 3 or 4 days. During the soaking, press down on the bag from time to time to help extract the color. After soaking, bring the bath to a boil and allow it to boil vigorously for 2 hours. Add water to the pan when necessary, and keep the pan covered to help reduce evaporation. After boiling, remove the cheesecloth bag with the sandalwood and add enough water to make 1 quart of dye. For each ounce of yarn to be dyed according to any of the following recipes, 1 quart of dye must be prepared.

## 20. Sandalwood on Unmordanted Yarn (Light Red)

1 quart dyebath
2 skeins unmordanted wool (1/2 ounce each)

Place the 2 wet skeins of unmordanted yarn in 1 quart of dyebath and simmer gently for 1 hour. Remove the skeins and rinse thoroughly. The yarn will be a light red.

## 21. Sandalwood with Alum (Red-Orange)

1 quart dyebath
2 skeins alum-mordanted wool (1/2 ounce each)

Place the 2 wet skeins of alum-mordanted yarn in 1 quart of dyebath and simmer gently for 1 hour. Remove the skeins and rinse thoroughly. The skeins will be a red-orange color. A deeper shade will be achieved if the skeins are allowed to cool in the bath before rinsing.

## 22. Sandalwood with Chrome (Red-Brown)

1 quart dyebath
2 skeins chrome-mordanted wool (1/2 ounce each)

Place the 2 wet skeins of chrome-mordanted yarn in 1 quart of dyebath and simmer gently for an hour. Remove the skeins and rinse thoroughly. The skeins will be a rich red-brown color that can be deepened by allowing the skeins to cool in the bath before rinsing.

## 23. Sandalwood with Tin and Cream of Tartar (Red)

1 quart dyebath
2 skeins unmordanted wool (1/2 ounce each)
1/16 teaspoon tin
1/8 teaspoon cream of tartar

Place the 2 wet skeins of unmordanted yarn in 1 quart of dyebath and simmer gently for 45 minutes. Remove the skeins and set them aside. Dissolve 1/16 teaspoon tin and 1/8 teaspoon cream of tartar in 1/4 cup water and add this to the dyebath, stirring to distribute it evenly. Replace the dyed skeins in the bath and simmer for 15 minutes more. Allow the skeins to cool in the dyebath and then rinse, first in soapy water and then in clear water. The yarn will be red, and brighter in intensity than the colors in the previous recipes.

# Brazilwood
## RED TO PURPLE

The brazilwood in use today is obtained from redwood trees known botanically as *Caesalpina echinata*. Several other trees, especially sapan and peachwood, were used in the past to obtain red dyes. Sapan was once an important item of trade from India and Ceylon to the countries of Europe.

The name brazilwood comes from the Arabic word *braza,* meaning "bright red." About 1500 A.D., traders who first landed on the northern part of the South American continent found great forests of redwood trees and gave the name "Terra de Brazil" to the area. Today Brazil is the leading supplier of the dyewood from which it derived its name. Dyers of old used brazilwood as an additive to heighten the color of madder, or as a substitute for cochineal to dye cheap scarlet cloth. It was also used in colonial times to make red writing ink.

The dyestuff is found in the heartwood of medium-sized redwood trees. The wood is a brownish red, and it yields its best colors if it is chipped into small pieces and allowed to soak for a week before using. Brazilwood chips may be purchased from dye supply houses.

### Preparing the Dyebath

1 ounce brazilwood chips
1 quart water

Tie 1 ounce of brazilwood chips in a cheesecloth bag and soak it in 1 quart of water. Although the bath may be used after soaking overnight or for several days, the amount of color obtained will be much greater if the chips are allowed to soak a full week. After soaking, bring the chips and water to a boil and let them boil vigorously for an hour. If the pan is covered during the boiling, there will be less evaporation from the bath. After boiling, remove the cheesecloth bag and add enough water to the bath to bring it up to a full quart. This dyebath may be used for any of the following recipes. For each ounce of yarn to be dyed, 1 quart of dyebath must be prepared.

## 24. Brazilwood on Unmordanted Yarn (Red-Lavender)

1 quart dyebath
2 skeins unmordanted wool (1/2 ounce each)

Place the 2 wet skeins of unmordanted yarn in 1 quart of dyebath and simmer gently for 45 minutes. Move the skeins around in the dyebath from time to time to assure even dyeing. After the yarn has simmered for 45 minutes, remove the skeins and rinse them thoroughly. The yarn will be a reddish lavender color.

## 25. Brazilwood with Alum (Crimson)

1 quart dyebath
2 skeins alum-mordanted wool (1/2 ounce each)

Heat 1 quart of dyebath to 180°F. In a separate container, warm the 2 alum-mordanted skeins in warm water. Place the wet skeins in the heated dyebath and simmer gently for 45 minutes. Remove the skeins and rinse thoroughly. The skeins are a clear crimson color. If a lighter color is desired, a shorter simmering time of 30 minutes could be used. Another way to obtain lighter colors is to use the same dyebath to dye more yarn.

## 26. Brazilwood with Chrome (Purple)

1 quart dyebath
2 skeins chrome-mordanted wool (1/2 ounce each)

Place the 2 wet skeins of chrome-mordanted yarn in the dyebath and simmer for 45 minutes. Remove the skeins and rinse them thoroughly. When dry, the skeins will be a strong purple color. If a lighter color is desired, shorten the simmering time. If a deeper shade is desired, the yarn may be left to cool in the bath overnight and then rinsed the next day. This same dyebath may be used to obtain lighter colors.

## 27. Brazilwood with Tin (Pink)

1 quart dyebath
2 skeins unmordanted wool (1/2 ounce each)
1/16 teaspoon tin

Place the 2 wet skeins of unmordanted yarn in 1 quart of dyebath and simmer gently for 30 minutes. Remove the skeins and set them aside. Dissolve 1/16 teaspoon tin in 1/4 cup of water and add this to the dyebath, stirring to assure even distribution. Replace the skeins and simmer an additional 15 minutes. Remove the skeins and rinse them, first in soapy water and then in clear water. The skeins will be a pink color.

## 28. Brazilwood with Baking Soda (Blue-Lavender)

1 quart dyebath
2 skeins unmordanted wool (1/2 ounce each)
1/2 teaspoon baking soda

Place the 2 wet skeins of unmordanted yarn in 1 quart of dyebath and simmer for 30 minutes. Remove the skeins and set them aside. Dissolve 1/2 teaspoon baking soda in 1/4 cup water and add this to the dyebath, stirring to distribute it evenly. Replace the two skeins and simmer for an additional 15 minutes. Remove the skeins and rinse them thoroughly. The skeins are a lavender color, inclining more toward blue because of the action of the baking soda. If either alum- or chrome-mordanted skeins are used instead of the unmordanted skeins, further variations of color can be obtained.

## 29. Brazilwood with Alum plus Copper Sulfate (Ruby)

1 quart dyebath
2 skeins alum-mordanted wool (1/2 ounce each)
1/4 teaspoon copper sulfate

Heat the dyebath quickly over a high heat until it reaches 180°F. While the bath is heating, warm the two skeins of alum-mordanted yarn in water until they are close to the temperature of the dyebath. Place the warmed skeins in the brazilwood bath and simmer for 30 minutes. Dissolve 1/4 teaspoon copper sulfate in 1/4 cup water. Lift the skeins out of the dyebath and stir in the dissolved copper sulfate. Replace the skeins in the bath and simmer an additional 15 minutes. Remove the skeins and rinse them thoroughly. The yarn will be a dull ruby color.

# Alkanet
## RED-GRAY TO BLUE-GRAY

The alkanet plant (*Alkanna tinctoria* or *Anchusa tinctoria*) has been used since antiquity for its red coloring. Pliny mentions its use for dyeing wool, and both Greek and Egyptian women are known to have painted their cheeks with it. In the Middle Ages the root of alkanet was boiled with wine and sweet butter to make what was called "red butter," prescribed as a remedy for a bad fall or as a cure for smallpox or measles. In America, the Indians used a variety of alkanets as a coloring for body paint.

Alkanet plants are perennials that produce clear blue flowers. The dye is contained in the roots, which range in color from a red to a purple depending on the variety of alkanet. The roots should be chopped and then soaked prior to using. Acids, such as vinegar or oxalic acid, will help produce a red color while alkalies will give a blue tone. The different varieties of alkanet will also influence the red or blue tones produced. Alkanet roots may be purchased from dye supply houses or the plants may be grown in your own garden.

### Preparing the Dyebath

1 ounce alkanet root

1 quart water

Chop the alkanet root into small pieces and put it in 1 quart of water to soak overnight. The next day, bring the bath to a boil and allow it to boil vigorously for 1 hour. Be sure to add a little water from time to time as it evaporates. After boiling, remove the alkanet and add enough water to make 1 quart of dye. For each ounce of yarn to be dyed in any of the following recipes, 1 quart of dye must be prepared.

### 30. Alkanet Root with Vinegar (Red-Gray)

1 quart dyebath
2 skeins unmordanted wool (1/2 ounce each)
1/3 cup white vinegar

Place the 2 wet skeins of unmordanted yarn in 1 quart of dyebath to which 1/3 cup white vinegar has been added. Simmer the yarn gently for 45 minutes. Remove the skeins and rinse thoroughly. The skeins will be gray with subdued red tones.

### 31. Alkanet Root with Alum (Gray)

1 quart dyebath
2 skeins alum-mordanted wool (1/2 ounce each)

Place the 2 wet skeins of alum-mordanted yarn in 1 quart of dyebath and simmer gently for 45 minutes. Remove the skeins and rinse thoroughly. The yarn will be a medium gray and may have warm overtones of red if the roots of the alkanet were rich in red coloring.

### 32. Alkanet Root with Oxalic Acid and Cream of Tartar (Purple-Gray)

1 quart dyebath
2 skeins unmordanted wool (1/2 ounce each)
1/3 cup white vinegar
1/4 teaspoon oxalic acid
1/2 teaspoon cream of tartar

Place the 2 wet skeins of unmordanted yarn in 1 quart of dyebath to which 1/3 cup of white vinegar has been added. Simmer the skeins for 30 minutes. Remove the skeins and set aside. Dissolve 1/4 teaspoon oxalic acid and 1/2 teaspoon cream of tartar in 1/4 cup of water and add to the dyebath, stirring to distribute it evenly. Replace the dyed skeins and simmer for an additional 15 minutes. Allow the skeins to cool in the bath and then rinse thoroughly. The skeins will be a purple-gray.

## 33. Alkanet Root with Baking Soda (Blue-Gray)

1 quart dyebath

2 skeins unmordanted wool (1/2 ounce each)

1/2 teaspoon baking soda

Place the 2 wet skeins of unmordanted yarn in 1 quart of dyebath and simmer gently for 30 minutes. Remove the skeins and set them aside. Add 1/2 teaspoon baking soda to the dyebath and stir until the baking soda is completely dissolved. Replace the dyed skeins in the bath and simmer for an additional 15 minutes. Allow the skeins to cool in the bath and then rinse thoroughly. The skeins are a medium gray with blue overtones.

# Orchil Lichens
## PURPLE

Lichens have been used since at least the time of the early Egyptians—they ate them, made dyes from them, and even used them to stuff the cavities of their mummies. Lichens are an interesting type of plant, for they are composed of fungi and algae living together in an association called "symbiosis." The fungus makes up the greater part of the lichen body and feeds on the food manufactured by the algae. Many lichens contain acids that, when treated properly, will produce a variety of dye colors. Of particular interest here are the lichens called orchils because they will give colors in the purple range.

The type of orchil lichen used at the time of the ancient Greeks was in all probability the "lichen roccella," which grew on rocks along the coastal shores of the Mediterranean. It was said to have been used as a base for the more expensive Tyrian purple (a dye made from the glands of shellfish). Following the decline of the Roman Empire, the orchil dye was temporarily forgotten.

About 1300 A.D., however, a Florentine dye merchant named Federigo by chance rediscovered the method of extracting color from the lichens along the Eastern Mediterranean coast. When broken pieces of orchil lichens are subjected to the effects of human urine, the acids in the lichens yield a red to reddish purple color. Federigo brought his secret home to Florence, and for many years he had a flourishing trade exporting orchil dyepaste. The Italian monopoly lasted for several centuries until the lichen was discovered along the West African coast and the secret of its preparation made its way to England.

In the eighteenth century, a Scottish chemist from Glasgow patented a dye compound made of several different lichens found in the British Isles. This preparation came to be known as cudbear, a name derived from the given name of the chemist, Dr. Cuthbert Gordon. The making of cudbear as an orchil-producing dyestuff has persisted to the present day, but it is not readily available to the amateur dyer.

One of the three lichens used for cudbear is of the Umbilicaria lichen family, which is a leafy or foliose lichen. Various types of these Umbilicaria are found today in many parts of the world—from Alaska to Florida and from Norway to New Zealand. The name "Umbilicaria" is derived from the fact that the lichen attaches itself to the surface of exposed rocks by means of one central cord. The lichens, which range from one to ten inches, are leathery in appearance and are either smooth or blistered on the surface. The color of the underside ranges from a light gray to a thick black.

Although they are not available commercially, Umbilicaria can be gathered if you are careful to follow conservation measures. Bear in mind that a lichen takes 30 to 40 years to reach full growth. Two ounces of powdered lichen will yield enough dye to give color to a pound of wool. Since Umbilicaria grow on the surfaces of exposed rocks, it is best to gather pieces which have broken off and lie at the base of the rocks.

The dye potential is contained in the acids found in the inner part of the lichen. A simple test will tell if a lichen has the orchil dye possibility. With a sharp knife or razor blade, carefully scrape away the thin outer layer of the upper surface of the lichen and expose a small area of the white underlayer. Place a tiny drop of household bleach (such as Clorox) on this white spot. If an orchil-producing acid is present, this spot will show a red or red-orange color on contact with the bleach.

## Preparing the Dyebath

1 ounce Umbilicaria lichen
2 tablespoons clear non-sudsy ammonia
4 tablespoons water

Crumble 1 ounce of lichen into small pieces with a mortar and pestel. The more the lichen is crumbled, the easier it will be to extract the acid from the inner areas. Mix 2 tablespoons of clear, non-sudsy ammonia with 4 table-spoons water. Put the crumbled lichen in a small glass jar and stir in about 1/2 of the ammonia-water solution. Keep adding a little more of the solution until the lichen is a stirrable thick paste. Cover the jar tightly and store it at room temperature out of direct sunlight.

For the next 3 days the mixture should be stirred several times a day. If it becomes too thick to stir, add a little ammonia-water solution. If you need more solution than you have prepared, then make more, maintaining a ratio of 2 parts of water to 1 part of ammonia. By the fourth or fifth day, the lichen solution should become a little runny and need be stirred only once or twice a day. By the tenth day there should be a dark, almost black liquid that becomes purple by the end of 2 weeks. The dye may be used at this time, but a stronger dye will result if it is left to ferment for 28 days. At the end of the fermentation period, leave the cover off the jar and allow the excess moisture to evaporate. The dry powder that remains may then be stored in the same jar for future use.

### 34. Umbilicaria on Unmordanted Yarn (Orchid)

1 teaspoon Umbilicaria dye powder

1 quart water

2 skeins unmordanted wool (1/2 ounce each)

Mix 1 teaspoonful Umbilicaria powder in 1 quart of water, stirring to make an even dyebath. Place the 2 wet skeins of unmordanted yarn in the dyebath and bring it slowly to the simmering point over medium heat. Simmer the yarn gently for 30 minutes. The yarn may be rinsed immediately, but the color will be deeper and more stable if the yarn is allowed to cool in the dyebath. The skeins will be orchid.

### 35. Umbilicaria with Alum (Red-Orchid)

1 teaspoon Umbilicaria powder

1 quart water

2 skeins alum-mordanted wool (1/2 ounce each)

Mix 1 teaspoon of Umbilicaria powder in 1 quart of water and stir to make an even dye. Place the 2 wet skeins of alum-mordanted yarn in the dyebath and bring the bath slowly to the simmering point over medium heat. Simmer gently for 30 minutes and allow the skeins to cool overnight in the bath. The next day take the skeins out and rinse them thoroughly. The color will be an orchid that inclines toward red.

### 36. Umbilicaria with Chrome Afterbath (Blue-Purple)

1 teaspoon Umbilicaria powder

1 quart water

2 skeins unmordanted wool (1/2 ounce each)

1/16 teaspoon chrome

1 quart water

Mix 1 teaspoon Umbilicaria powder in 1 quart water and stir to make an even dyebath. Place the 2 wet skeins of unmordanted yarn in the dyebath and heat it slowly to the simmering point. Simmer gently for 30 minutes. Dissolve 1/16 teaspoon chrome in 1/4 cup water and add this to 1 quart of water in a separate pan from the dyebath. Heat the chrome bath to the simmering point, then add the dyed skeins. Simmer for 15 minutes and then allow the skeins to cool in the bath overnight. The next day remove the skeins and rinse them thoroughly. The skeins will be a purple inclining toward blue. The chrome afterbath helps make the Umbilicaria a more stable color. If chrome-mordanted skeins had been used, the yarn would have been a darker, saddened orchid.

### 37. Umbilicaria with Baking Soda (Blue-Orchid)

1 teaspoon Umbilicaria powder

1 quart water

2 skeins unmordanted wool (1/2 ounce each)

1/2 teaspoon baking soda

Mix 1 teaspoon Umbilicaria powder in 1 quart water and stir to make an even dye. Place the 2 wet skeins of unmordanted yarn in the dyebath and bring the bath slowly to the simmering point. Simmer for 30 minutes. Remove the skeins and set them aside. Dissolve 1/2 teaspoon baking soda in 1/4 cup water and add it to the dyebath, stirring to distribute it evenly. Replace the skeins and simmer for an additional 15 minutes. Allow the skeins to cool in the dyebath and then rinse thoroughly. The skeins will be orchid with blue overtones due to the alkali content of the baking soda.

### 38. Umbilicaria with Vinegar (Red-Orchid)

1 teaspoon Umbilicaria powder

1 quart water

2 skeins unmordanted wool (1/2 ounce each)

1/4 cup white vinegar

Mix 1 teaspoon of Umbilicaria powder in 1 quart of water and stir thoroughly. Place the 2 wet skeins of unmordanted yarn in the dyebath and slowly raise the temperature to the simmering point. Simmer for 30 minutes. Remove the skeins and set them aside. Add 1/4 cup white vinegar to the dyebath and stir to make an even bath. Replace the dyed skeins in the bath and simmer for an additional 15 minutes. Allow the skeins to cool in the dyebath and then rinse them thoroughly. The skeins will change from an orchid to a red-orchid because of the action of the acetic acid in the vinegar.

Note: You may find that the Umbilicaria powder will not completely dissolve in these dyebaths. Any tiny particles that cling to the yarn will easily shake off when the yarn is rinsed. The dyebaths are also still capable of dyeing at least several more skeins of wool before the color is exhausted. Lighter colors will result from successive baths.

Umbilicaria-dyed skeins are not fast to direct sunlight, but do preserve much of their color when protected from direct exposure. One of the uses for the umbilicaria dyebath is to heighten or "bloom" colors made from another dye material. For example: a skein that has been dyed with madder and then put into an Umbilicaria bath will have an added luster and a more vibrant color.

# Logwood
## VIOLET TO BLACK

Logwood (*Haematoxylon campechianum*) is a small, many-trunked redwood tree that was named by the Spaniards who discovered it on the shores of the Bay of Campeche in Mexico. Logwood was introduced to Europe in the sixteenth century, but was soon banned in Britain as a fugitive dye. The ban was repealed about 100 years later when the proper use of mordants made it a truly stable dye.

In colonial America it was thought of as a very valuable dye, both because it produced a number of colors and because it was an inexpensive dye material. In 1831, logwood was one of the six principal imported dye materials and sold for 6¢ a pound. It was especially prized because it could produce a good black when used with iron as a mordant.

The dye is contained in the heartwood of the tree. First the trunks are cut and stripped of their bark. They are then exported from the tropical areas of America as large logs, which are later chipped or pulverized. As Bronson wrote in *Weaving and Dyeing* in 1817, "The best of it is very hard, compact, heavy and of a red color." Logwood may be purchased from dye supply houses as small chips or as a fine powder.

### Preparing the Dyebath

1 ounce logwood chips or powder
1 quart water

Tie 1 ounce of logwood chips or powder in a small cheesecloth bag and soak overnight in 1 quart of water. The next day bring the bath to a boil and allow it to boil vigorously for 60 minutes. Remove the bag with the logwood and add enough water to make 1 quart of dye. For each ounce of yarn to be dyed according to any of the following recipes, 1 quart of dyebath must be prepared.

### 39. Logwood with Alum (Deep Purple)

1 quart dyebath
2 skeins alum-mordanted wool (1/2 ounce each)

Place the 2 wet skeins of alum-mordanted yarn in 1 quart of dyebath and simmer for 45 minutes. Remove the skeins and rinse them thoroughly. The yarn will be a deep purple.

### 40. Logwood with Alum plus Tin (Purple)

1 quart dyebath
2 skeins alum-mordanted wool (1/2 ounce each)
1/16 teaspoon tin

Place the 2 wet skeins of alum-mordanted yarn in 1 quart of dyebath and simmer for 30 minutes. Remove the skeins and set them aside. Dissolve 1/16 teaspoon tin in 1/4 cup water and add this to the dyebath, stirring to distribute it evenly. Replace the dyed skeins in the bath and simmer for an additional 15 minutes. Remove the skeins and rinse, first in soapy water and then in clear water. The skeins will be purple, but lighter than the color produced in the previous recipe.

### 41. Logwood with Chrome (Navy Blue)

1 quart dyebath
2 skeins chrome-mordanted wool (1/2 ounce each)

Place the 2 wet skeins of chrome-mordanted yarn in the 1 quart of dyebath and simmer for 45 minutes. Remove the skeins and rinse thoroughly. The skeins will be a dark navy blue.

### 42. Logwood with Chrome plus Iron (Blue-Black)

1 quart dyebath
2 skeins chrome-mordanted wool (1/2 ounce each)
1/16 teaspoon iron

Place the 2 wet skeins of chrome-mordanted yarn in 1 quart of dyebath and simmer for 30 minutes. Remove the skeins and set them aside. Dissolve 1/16 teaspoon iron in 1/4 cup water and add this to the dyebath, stirring to distribute it evenly. Replace the dyed skeins and simmer for an additional 15 minutes. Allow the skeins to cool in the dyebath, then rinse, first in soapy water and then in clear water. The yarn will be a dark blue-black.

### 43. Logwood with Tin (Violet)

1 quart dyebath
2 skeins unmordanted wool (1/2 ounce each)
1/16 teaspoon tin

Place the 2 wet skeins of unmordanted yarn in the 1 quart of dyebath and simmer gently for 30 minutes. Remove the skeins and set them aside. Dissolve 1/16 teaspoon tin in 1/4 cup of water and add this to the dyebath, stirring to distribute it evenly. Replace the dyed skeins in the bath and simmer for an additional 15 minutes. Allow the skeins to cool in the bath and then rinse, first in soapy water and then in clear water. The skeins will be a violet color that is lighter than any produced in the previous recipes.

### 44. Logwood with Alum plus Baking Soda (Blue-Purple)

1 quart dyebath
2 skeins alum-mordanted wool (1/2 ounce each)
1/2 teaspoon baking soda

Dissolve 1/2 teaspoon baking soda in 1/4 cup of water and add it to 1 quart of dyebath, stirring to distribute it evenly. Place the 2 wet skeins of alum-mordanted yarn in the logwood-baking soda dyebath and simmer gently for 45 minutes. Allow the skeins to cool in the dyebath and then rinse them thoroughly. The skeins will be dark purple with blue overtones.

### 45. Logwood with Copper Sulfate (Black)

1 quart dyebath
2 skeins unmordanted wool (1/2 ounce each)
1/2 teaspoon copper sulfate

Place the 2 wet skeins of unmordanted yarn in the 1 quart of dyebath and simmer gently for 30 minutes. Remove the skeins and set them aside. Dissolve 1/2 teaspoon copper sulfate in 1/4 cup water and add this to the dyebath, stirring to distribute it evenly. Replace the dyed skeins in the bath and simmer for an additional 15 minutes. Allow the skeins to cool in the dyebath and then rinse thoroughly. The yarn will be black.

Note: All of the dyebaths mentioned still have enough dye potential to dye other skeins of yarn. The colors will be lighter or weaker than the ones achieved initially.

# *Indigo*
## BLUE

The indigo plant is a member of the pea or legume family, and its dye is one of the most highly prized. Evidence of its use in antiquity has been found in many cultures all over the world. It was used not only as a dye for cloth but also as a cosmetic coloring. The name "indigo" is derived from the Latin word *indicum,* meaning " from India." There are several varieties of the indigo plant, but the one most widely used in antiquity was *Indigo tinctoria,* which was exported principally from India.

There are also several varieties of the indigo plant in the Americas, and the Indians were using them for dye at the time of the Spanish discoveries. The name "anil," which they used to designate indigo, comes from the Spanish *al-nil,* meaning "blue." During colonial times indigo was cultivated in the Southeastern United States where *indigo suffruticosa* still grows today.

The dye potential is contained in the leaves of the indigo plant, which when allowed to ferment and then oxidize produce a blue powder that is insoluble in water. In *Elements of the Art of Dyeing* by Bertollet, published in 1824, there is a fine description of the method used to precipitate the blue dye powder. The plants are harvested when they reach maturity and then put into vats of water to ferment. After a brisk fermentation has occurred, the yellowish green liquid is put into another vat where it is beaten to dissipate the gas and to combine oxygen with the coloring matter. As this oxidization occurs, the liquid in the vat becomes a deep blue color. It is then permitted to rest for a few hours to allow the insoluble dye particles to settle to the bottom of the vat. The top liquid is drawn off and the remaining liquid strained through a fine cloth. The blue solid matter that remains is placed in boxes and allowed to dry before being cut into squares or powdered. Bronson, in 1817, noted that Bengal indigo (which he considered the best) was available for sale in pieces two inches square. Today indigo powder may be purchased from dye supply houses. When ordering, be sure to specify that you want the natural indigo powder and not a synthetic.

There are a number of ways of preparing the indigo bath or changing the insoluble blue powder to a greenish yellow water-soluble solution). Once this is done, the yarn is dipped in the dye bath, and when drawn out is a greenish yellow color. As the yarn is exposed to the air, the coloring matter unites with oxygen, and this oxidation turns the yarn to blue. Repeated dippings and airings serve to deepen the color produced.

The insoluble blue powder can be changed by the use of sulfuric acid, however it is at best a dangerous chemical to use and not for the amateur dyer. Another method uses fresh green vitriol, madder, and wheat bran. A traditional Indian method of using indigo was to collect the urine of the children in a large pot placed outside. Because of the warm climate, the urine fermented in about two weeks. The indigo powder was then placed in the fermented urine, which caused it to begin to dissolve. The mixture was kept warm and the yarn to be dyed was immersed in the warm fluid. When taken out and aired, the yarn assumed a blue color. This method is sometimes used today, but the fermented urine does produce a strong odor.

After reviewing many ways to produce an indigo bath, the following is offered as the easiest method, with a minimum of dangerous chemicals and little truly offensive odor.

## Preparing the Dyebath

1/2 ounce indigo powder
1 ounce washing soda
1 quart warm water
2 ounces sodium hydrosulfite

Put 1/2 ounce indigo powder in a small enamel pan and add 1/4 cup warm water. Stir to form a paste. In a separate jar combine 1 ounce washing soda and 4 ounces of water, and stir until the washing soda is completely dissolved. Add 2-1/2 ounces of the fluid washing soda to the indigo paste in the saucepan and stir thoroughly. Shake in 1 ounce of the sodium hydrosulfite and stir. Add 1 quart of warm water and stir gently to make an even bath. Heat the mixture of 130°F. (Take care not to exceed 140°F. or the solution will not work.) The liquid in the saucepan should begin to turn a yellowish color. Now let the liquid stand for 20 minutes, after which the color should be a yellow-green. Shake 1 ounce of the sodium hydrosulfite over the surface of the saucepan to render harmless any dissolved oxygen. The dyebath is now ready to use.

## 46. Indigo on Unmordanted Yarn (Blue)

1 quart indigo dyebath
2 skeins of unmordanted wool (1/2 ounce each)

Warm the 1 quart of dyebath to 130°F. Wet the yarn thoroughly in warm water and then submerge it completely in the dyebath. Do not agitate the bath to avoid adding oxygen to it. Leave the skeins in for a few minutes and then remove them, carefully squeezing out the excess dye liquid. As the skeins come out of the bath they are a yellow-green color but will begin to turn blue when exposed to the air. In 15 or 20 minutes the skeins should be completely blue. Allow one skein to dry completely and then rinse it thoroughly until the water is clear. To achieve a deeper color on the other skein, dip it in the bath again and air it for another 15 or 20 minutes. Repeated dippings and airings will deepen the color even further. After attaining the desired color, rinse the skein thoroughly until the water is clear.

This dyebath will serve to dye many skeins of yarn and may be kept successfully for weeks. If a blue coating settles on the surface of the bath, shake 1/2 ounce of sodium hydrosulfite over it before using. Alum-mordanted skeins may be used instead of unmordanted ones without appreciably dulling the blue color achieved. The indigo dyebath is especially helpful when overdyeing to produce greens and purples.

# 4.
# Yellows
# Golds
# Oranges

# *Fustic*
## YELLOW

Historically, the dye known as fustic was produced from two different plants. Young fustic, also called Venetian sumac, was derived from the branches of the smoke tree (*Rhus cotinus*). This shrublike tree is native to southern Europe and Asia and has been known since the time of the Roman Empire. Young fustic as a dye is not readily available today, but the so-called "old" fustic is.

Old fustic is made from a tree of the mulberry family (*Chlorophora tinctoria*) that grows wild in the tropical areas of the Americas. The dye is found in the inner wood of the trunk of the tree. It can be purchased as small pieces of wood or as an extract. It is best to shave the wood into slivers and to soak it for at least 24 hours before using. This procedure will yield a clearer and brighter yellow, as too long a boiling time tends to dull the color. The colors will range from a bright yellow to a golden or greenish yellow depending on the mordant used.

### Preparing the Dyebath

1 ounce chopped fustic

1 quart water

Tie the chopped fustic in a small cheesecloth bag. Soak the bag in 1 quart of water for at least 24 hours. Heat the fustic and water over medium heat until it reaches the boiling point and simmer gently for 45 minutes. Do not allow the bath to boil vigorously or the excessive heat will dull the color. At the end of the simmering time, remove the cheesecloth bag with the fustic wood and add enough water to the bath to make 1 quart of dyebath. For any one of the following recipes for fustic dye, 1 quart of dyebath should be prepared.

## 47. Fustic with Alum (Golden Yellow)

1 quart dyebath
2 skeins alum-mordanted wool (1/2 ounce each)

Place the 2 wet skeins of alum-mordanted yarn in 1 quart of dyebath. Bring the bath to the simmering point and let it simmer gently for 30 minutes. Remove both skeins and rinse until the water is clear. The yarn will be a golden yellow.

## 48. Fustic with Alum plus Tin (Bright Yellow)

1 quart dyebath
2 skeins alum-mordanted wool (1/2 ounce each)
1/16 teaspoon tin

Using 1 quart of dye, place the 2 wet skeins of alum-mordanted wool in the dyebath and simmer for 30 minutes. Remove both skeins and set them aside. Dissolve 1/16 teaspoon tin in 1/4 cup of water and add it to the dyebath, stirring to distribute it evenly. Place the 2 skeins back in the bath and simmer gently for an additional 15 minutes. Remove the skeins and rinse, first in soapy water and then in clear water. The skeins will be a sharp bright yellow instead of a golden yellow.

## 49. Fustic with Chrome (Deep Gold)

1 quart dyebath
2 skeins chrome-mordanted wool (1/2 ounce each)
Place the 2 wet skeins of chrome-mordanted yarn in 1 quart of dyebath. Bring the bath to the simmering point and let it simmer for 30 minutes. Remove both skeins and rinse them until the water is clear. The yarn will be a deeper gold than produced in Recipe 47.

## 50. Fustic with Copper Sulfate (Greenish Yellow)

1 quart dyebath

2 skeins unmordanted wool (1/2 ounce each)

1/2 teaspoon copper sulfate

Using 1 quart of dyebath, place the 2 wet skeins of unmordanted yarn in the dyebath and simmer for 30 minutes. Remove both skeins and set them aside. Dissolve 1/2 teaspoon copper sulfate in 1/4 cup warm water. Add this to the dyebath, stirring to distribute it evenly. Place the dyed skeins back in the bath and simmer for an additional 15 minutes. Remove the skeins and rinse thoroughly. The color of the yarn has changed from a dull brownish yellow to a greenish yellow. Alum-mordanted or chrome-mordanted skeins could also be used in the copper sulfate bath. The color would be a brighter greenish yellow with the alum-mordanted skeins and a deeper greenish yellow with the chrome-mordanted skeins.

# *Saffron*
## YELLOW

Saffron (*Crocus sativus*) should not be confused with the spring blooming crocus (*Crocus vernis*). The bulbs or corms of *Crocus sativus* are planted in early summer. Purple flowers, about four inches high, appear in the fall and are followed by long slender leaves. The dried orange stigma from the pistils of the flowers are used as both a medicinal and cooking herb, as well as for coloring food and textiles. The name "saffron" is derived from the Arabic word for the color, *za'faran*.

Saffron is mentioned frequently in Greek and Roman literature as well as in the biblical Songs of Solomon. The Greeks considered it to be not only an important dyestuff, but a color for royalty. The Romans used saffron water as a fragrance for their theaters. In the Middle Ages, saffron was a much-sought-after dye material in the trade centers of northern Italy and Switzerland. Among the cities to adopt the saffron blossom as part of a coat of arms was Basle, Switzerland, which exported saffron to northern Europe and England.

As a medieval medicinal herb, saffron was said to have great powers for clearing the lungs and chest of congestion and for restoring easy breathing to the sick. Today it is still used in cooking for its flavor and coloring potential. It is cultivated as a crop in Spain, France, and parts of the Near East. As soon as the flowers open in late summer or fall, they are picked and the orange stigmas are plucked off and dried. Saffron may be purchased from dye supply houses and grocery stores (in Spanish groceries it may be less expensive than in regular supermarkets).

## Preparing the Dyebath

1/4 ounce saffron

1 quart water

Tie the saffron in a loosely woven cheesecloth bag and soak it in 1 quart of water for several hours or overnight. The soaking time helps to draw the color out of the saffron so the intensity of the color is not lost by excessive boiling. After it has soaked, heat the saffron and water to the boiling point and let it simmer gently for 30 minutes. By this time the bath should be a strong yellow-orange color. Remove the saffron from the dyebath. If necessary, add enough water to make 1 quart of dye. For each ounce of yarn to be dyed according to any one of the recipes, 1 quart of dyebath must be prepared.

## 51. Saffron on Unmordanted Yarn (Bright Yellow)

1 quart dyebath

2 skeins unmordanted wool (1/2 ounce each)

Place the 2 wet skeins of unmordanted yarn in the dyebath and simmer for 30 minutes. Remove the skeins from the dyebath and rinse them thoroughly. Dry them in a shady place. The yarn will be a bright, clear yellow.

## 52. Saffron with Alum (Yellow)

1 quart dyebath

2 skeins alum-mordanted wool (1/2 ounce each)

Place the 2 wet skeins of alum-mordanted yarn in the dyebath and simmer gently for 40 minutes. Remove the skeins from the bath, rinse them thoroughly, and dry in a shady place. The skeins will be a clear yellow, but not as intense as the color in Recipe 51.

## 53. Saffron with Chrome (Dull Yellow)

1 quart dyebath

2 skeins chrome-mordanted wool (1/2 ounce each)

Place the 2 wet skeins of chrome-mordanted yarn in the dyebath and simmer for 40 minutes. Remove the skeins from the bath and rinse thoroughly. Dry them in a shady place. The skeins will be a dull yellow color that lack the clarity shown in the previous recipes.

## 54. Saffron with Copper Sulfate (Yellow-Green)

1 quart dyebath
2 skeins unmordanted wool (1/2 ounce each)
1/2 teaspoon copper sulfate

Place the 2 wet skeins of unmordanted yarn in the dyebath and simmer gently for 30 minutes. Remove the skeins from the bath and set them aside. The skeins are now a bright yellow. Dissolve thoroughly 1/2 teaspoon copper sulfate in 1/4 cup of water and add this to the dyebath, stirring to distribute it evenly. Replace the dyed skeins in the bath and simmer an additional 20 minutes. Remove the skeins and rinse them well. The yarn has changed from a bright yellow to a sharp yellow-green. If a deeper shade is desired, increase the amount of copper sulfate to 3/4 teaspoon per quart of dyebath. If a lighter shade is desired, reduce the amount of copper sulfate to 1/4 teaspoon per quart of dyebath.

It should be noted that the addition of 1/16 teaspoon of tin per quart of dyebath would brighten or sharpen the colors in these recipes, just as the addition of 1/16 teaspoon of iron would darken or sadden them.

# Tumeric

## YELLOW

Turmeric (*Curcuma longa*), a perennial herb native to India and China, is sometimes called the Indian saffron plant. Turmeric has been used as a coloring agent, as a flavoring in curry powder and pickles, and as a stimulant in herbal medicine. Silk and wool were dyed with turmeric powder in Asia, Greece, and Rome. It has also been used as a dye to deepen the colors obtained by fustic or weld. In the Orient a scarlet color was produced by dyeing first with turmeric and then overdyeing with a dye made from safflower cakes.

The dye is obtained from the roots or tubers of the turmeric plant. Good roots will be hard with a dull, waxy surface. The deep orange-yellow color comes from the inner part of the tuber. To release the dye, the tubers should be pulverized or chopped fine and then soaked in water. During the soaking, press down on the turmeric with a spoon to help soften it and expose more of the coloring substance. Turmeric is available from dye supply houses as chopped tubers or from grocery stores as turmeric powder. If the turmeric powder is used to make a dyebath, be sure to dissolve it completely or particles may float on the surface of the dyebath and cause an uneven dye. The colors produced with turmeric range from a light yellow to a yellow-orange. They will fade in direct sunlight.

## Preparing the Dyebath with Tubers

1 ounce turmeric tubers

1 quart water

Chop 1 ounce of turmeric tubers into small pieces. The tubers are very hard and it may be necessary to pound them on a hard surface with a hammer. A nutcracker may also be used to crack them open. Unless the orange-yellow interior is sufficiently broken up, the dye potential will not be fully utilized.

Tie the chopped pieces in a cheesecloth bag and soak them in 1 quart of water for 36 to 48 hours. After soaking, place the turmeric and water over medium heat and bring it slowly to the boiling point. This should take about 30 minutes. Simmer the turmeric gently for 60 minutes (do not boil it or the color will be dulled). During the time the bath is heating and simmering, press down on the cheesecloth bag to release as much color as possible. After simmering, remove the bag with the turmeric and add enough water to make 1 quart of dye. Prepare 1 quart of dyebath for each ounce of wool to be dyed according to any of the following recipes.

## Preparing the Dyebath with Powder

1/2 ounce turmeric powder

1 quart water

Tie 1/2 ounce of turmeric powder loosely in a cheesecloth bag and soak it in 1 quart of water overnight. The next day bring the bath slowly to the boiling point and simmer it gently for 60 minutes. Using a spoon, press down on the cheesecloth bag to help release the color. At the end of 60 minutes, remove the cheesecloth bag and squeeze out as much dye as you can. Add enough water to make 1 quart of dye. For each ounce of yarn to be dyed according to any of the following recipes, 1 quart of dye must be prepared.

## 55. Turmeric on Unmordanted Yarn (Yellow)

1 quart dyebath

2 skeins unmordanted wool (1/2 ounce each)

Place the 2 wet skeins of unmordanted yarn in 1 quart of dyebath and simmer gently for 45 minutes. Remove the skeins and rinse them thoroughly. The yarn will be a light yellow. The color may be deepened by simmering an additional 20 minutes or more. The depth of the color can also be increased by allowing the yarn to cool in the dyebath overnight before rinsing.

### 56. Turmeric with Alum (Yellow)

1 quart dyebath

2 skeins alum-mordanted wool (1/2 ounce each)

Place the 2 wet skeins of alum-mordanted yarn in 1 quart of dyebath and simmer for 45 minutes. Remove the skeins and rinse them thoroughly. The color is a clear yellow. It may be deepened by simmering longer or by leaving the yarn to cool overnight in the dyebath before rinsing.

### 57. Turmeric with Chrome (Golden Yellow)

1 quart dyebath

2 skeins chrome-mordanted wool (1/2 ounce each)

Place the 2 wet skeins of chrome-mordanted yarn in 1 quart of dyebath and simmer gently for 60 minutes. Remove the skeins and rinse them thoroughly. The yarn will be a rich golden yellow.

### 58. Turmeric with Tin (Orange-Yellow)

1 quart dyebath

2 skeins unmordanted wool (1/2 ounce each)

1/16 teaspoon tin

Place the 2 wet skeins of unmordanted yarn in 1 quart of dyebath and simmer for 45 minutes. Remove the skeins and set them aside. Dissolve 1/16 teaspoon tin in 1/4 cup water and add this to the dyebath, stirring to distribute it evenly. Replace the skeins in the bath and simmer for an additional 15 minutes. Remove the skeins and rinse, first in soapy water and then in clear water. The skeins will be an orange-yellow because of the action of the tin.

### 59. Turmeric with Iron (Dull Yellow)

1 quart dyebath

2 skeins unmordanted wool (1/2 ounce each)

1/16 teaspoon iron

Place the 2 wet skeins of unmordanted yarn in 1 quart of dyebath and simmer gently for 45 minutes. Remove the skeins and set them aside. Dissolve 1/16 teaspoon iron in 1/4 cup water and add this to the dyebath, stirring to distribute it evenly. Replace the skeins in the bath and simmer for an additional 15 minutes. Remove the skeins and rinse, first in mild soapy water and then in clear water. The skeins will become a dull yellow because of the action of the iron.

### 60. Turmeric with Copper Sulfate (Bright Green)

1 quart dyebath
2 skeins unmordanted wool (1/2 ounce each)
1/2 teaspoon copper sulfate

Place the 2 wet skeins of unmordanted yarn in 1 quart of dyebath and simmer for 40 minutes. Remove the skeins and set them aside. Dissolve 1/2 teaspoon copper sulfate in 1/4 cup water and add this to the dyebath, stirring to distribute it evenly. Replace the yellow skeins in the dyebath and simmer for an additional 20 minutes. Remove the skeins and rinse them thoroughly. The skeins will be a bright green color because of the copper sulfate. For a lighter green, reduce the amount of copper sulfate to 1/4 teaspoon; for a deeper green, increase the copper sulfate to 3/4 teaspoon per quart of dyebath.

Note: In the recipes combining turmeric with tin, iron, and copper sulfate, the unmordanted yarn could be replaced with alum- or chrome-mordanted skeins. This would provide further gradations of color.

# Barberry

## YELLOW

The dye made from the barberry bush (*Berberis vulgaris*), a familiar border landscape plant, produces a strong yellow color. Thomas Cooper, in his treatise on dyeing published in 1815, said that dyers of Moroccan leather used barberry dye to mix with their cochineal dye. It is rich in natural mordants and helps to heighten both the life and intensity of a color. Both the green-leaved and the red-leaved barberry may be used with equal success.

The dye is contained in the inner wood of the stems and in the vivid yellow roots of mature plants. Both can be used either fresh or dried. If you are gathering in the fall, save the red berries separately to make a pale red dye. When using stems first remove the dark outer bark (be careful of the prickers) as this will produce a clearer yellow. The stems and the roots should be cut into small pieces to release the color. A good pencil sharpener is a handy way to make shavings of the smaller stems.

## Preparing the Dyebath

2 cups chopped barberry stems or roots

1-1/2 quarts water

Tie the 2 cups of chopped barberry in cheesecloth and soak it in 1-1/2 quarts of water for at least 3 days to help soften the wood. After soaking, bring water and barberry to the boiling point and simmer for 2 hours. Keep the pan covered to help reduce evaporation. Remove the barberry and measure the remaining liquid. If it is less than 1 quart, add enough water to make a quart of dye. For each ounce of yarn to be dyed according to any of the following recipes, 1 quart of dyebath must be prepared.

### 61. Barberry on Unmordanted Yarn (Bright Yellow)

1 quart dyebath
2 skeins unmordanted wool (1/2 ounce each)

Place the 2 wet skeins of unmordanted yarn in 1 quart of dyebath and simmer gently for 40 minutes. Leave the skeins to cool in the bath. When cool, rinse the skeins thoroughly. The yarn will be a bright clear yellow.

### 62. Barberry with Alum (Yellow)

1 quart dyebath
2 skeins alum-mordanted wool (1/2 ounce each)

Place the 2 wet skeins of alum-mordanted yarn in 1 quart of dyebath and simmer gently for 40 minutes. Allow the skeins to cool in the dyebath for a richer color. When cool, remove them and rinse thoroughly. The skeins will be yellow, but not as bright as those in Recipe 61.

### 63. Barberry with Chrome (Golden Yellow)

1 quart dyebath
2 skeins chrome-mordanted wool (1/2 ounce each)

Place the 2 wet skeins of chrome-mordanted yarn in 1 quart of dyebath and simmer gently for 40 minutes. Allow the skeins to cool in the dyebath for a deeper color. When cool, remove them and rinse thoroughly. The skeins will be a golden yellow color.

### 64. Barberry with Tin (Light Yellow)

1 quart dyebath
2 skeins unmordanted wool (1/2 ounce each)
1/16 teaspoon tin

Place the 2 wet skeins of unmordanted yarn in 1 quart of dyebath and simmer gently for 30 minutes. Remove the skeins and set them aside. Dissolve 1/16 teaspoon tin in 1/4 cup of water and add this to the dyebath, stirring to distribute it evenly. Replace the dyed skeins in the bath and simmer for an additional 15 minutes. Allow them to cool in the bath, then rinse, first in soapy water and then in clear water. The skeins will be a light, clear yellow.

## 65. Barberry with Iron (Green-Yellow)

1 quart dyebath
2 skeins unmordanted wool (1/2 ounce each)
1/16 teaspoon iron

Place the 2 wet skeins of unmordanted yarn in 1 quart of dyebath and simmer gently for 30 minutes. Remove the skeins and set them aside. Dissolve 1/16 teaspoon iron in 1/4 cup water and add this to the bath, stirring to distribute it evenly. Replace the dyed skeins in the bath and simmer an additional 15 minutes. Allow the skeins to cool in the bath and then rinse, first in soapy water and then in clear water. The skeins will be a saddened yellow with green overtones.

# *Weld*
## YELLOW

Weld (*Reseda Luteola*), also called dyers' mignonette or dyers' weed, is considered to be the oldest yellow dyestuff known to man. The Romans regarded weld as a color symbolizing purity and used the dye for bridal clothes and the garments of vestal virgins. During the Middle Ages it was grown and used throughout western Europe. At the time of the colonization of America it was a principal yellow dye for the English. In his 1815 treatise, Cooper says that to produce yellow one need only have weld, fustic, and quercitron (the bark from a species of oak tree).

Weld, an annual herb, grows to a height of three feet. The plants come into full bloom in June and July, and they should be gathered at this time. All parts of the plant except the roots can be used, but the upper parts of the stalks with the leaves and flowers or seeds are the richest in dye potential. The plants may be used fresh or air-dried for future use. The only disadvantage of using weld is that for every ounce of wool to be dyed, at least three ounces of weld should be used. Depending on the mordants used, colors ranging from bright yellow to gold to yellow-green may be produced. A fine medium green can be achieved by using weld followed by an indigo overdye.

## Preparing the Dyebath

3 ounces weld

1 quart water

Break the 3 ounces of weld stalks into small pieces and tie them in a cheesecloth bag. Put this in 1 quart of water to soak for 3 or 4 hours. Bring the bath to the boiling point and simmer for 45 minutes. Remove the weld from the bath and add enough water to make 1 quart of dye. For each ounce of yarn to be dyed according to any of the following recipes, 1 quart of dye must be prepared.

### 66. Weld with Alum (Yellow)

1 quart dyebath
2 skeins alum-mordanted wool (1/2 ounce each)

Place the 2 wet skeins of alum-mordanted yarn in 1 quart of dyebath and simmer gently for 30 minutes. Allow the skeins to cool in the dyebath and then rinse thoroughly. The yarn will be a rich clear yellow.

### 67. Weld with Chrome (Gold)

1 quart dyebath
2 skeins chrome-mordanted wool (1/2 ounce each)

Place the 2 wet skeins of chrome-mordanted yarn in 1 quart of dyebath and simmer gently for 30 minutes. Allow the skeins to cool in the bath and then rinse thoroughly. The yarn will be a lustrous gold color.

### 68. Weld with Tin (Bright Yellow)

1 quart dyebath
2 skeins unmordanted wool (1/2 ounce each)
1/16 teaspoon tin
1/8 teaspoon cream of tartar

Place the 2 wet skeins of unmordanted yarn in 1 quart of dyebath and simmer for 30 minutes. Remove the skeins and set them aside. Dissolve 1/16 teaspoon tin and 1/8 teaspoon cream of tartar in 1/4 cup of water. Add this to the dyebath, stirring to assure even distribution. Replace the dyed skeins in the bath and simmer for an additional 15 minutes. Allow the skeins to cool in the dyebath and then rinse, first in soapy water and then in clear water. The skeins will be a bright yellow.

## 69. Weld with Alum plus Copper Sulfate and Baking Soda (Green-Gold)

1 quart dyebath
2 skeins alum-mordanted wool (1/2 ounce each)
1/2 teaspoon copper sulfate
1/2 teaspoon baking soda

Place the 2 wet skeins of alum-mordanted yarn in 1 quart of dyebath and simmer for 30 minutes. Remove the skeins and set them aside. Dissolve 1/2 teaspoon copper sulfate and 1/2 teaspoon baking soda in 1/4 cup water. Add this to the dyebath, stirring to assure even distribution. Replace the dyed skeins in the bath and simmer for an additional 15 minutes. Allow the skeins to cool in the bath and then rinse thoroughly. The yarn will be gold with green overtones.

## 70. Weld with Alum plus Salt and Ammonia (Sharp Yellow)

1 quart dyebath
2 skeins alum-mordanted wool (1/2 ounce each)
2 teaspoons coarse unoxided salt
1/3 cup clear non-sudsy ammonia

Place the 2 wet skeins of alum-mordanted yarn in 1 quart of dyebath and simmer gently for 30 minutes. Remove the skeins and set them aside. Dissolve 2 teaspoons salt in the dyebath and then add 1/3 cup of clear non-sudsy ammonia. Replace the dyed skeins in the bath and simmer for an additional 15 minutes. Allow the skeins to cool in the dyebath and then rinse them thoroughly. The skeins will be a sharp yellow with the intensity heightened by the addition of the salt and ammonia.

# Safflower
## YELLOW-GOLD

Safflower (*Carthamus tinctorius*), a member of the thistle family, is also called American saffron or false saffron. It is a very ancient plant native to a large area—from central Asia through the Middle East to the upper Nile River into Ethiopia. It was used for food and medicine as well as for a dye on silk and linen. The tombs of Egypt are said to have contained cloth dyed with safflower.

The safflower plant grows to a height of about three feet. In June and July it produces the many red thistle-like flowers that are the sources of the dye. The flowers contain two colors, a water-soluble yellow and a red that has a greater affinity for vegetable fibers such as cotton and linen than for animal fibers such as wool. This red dye used to be combined with talcum powder and used for rouge. The dried petals of the safflower plant may be purchased from dye supply houses or the plants may be grown in a sunny spot in your own garden.

### Preparing the Dyebath for Gold

1 ounce safflower petals
1 quart water

Tie 1 ounce of safflower petals in a cheesecloth bag and soak it for 3 or 4 hours in 1 quart of water. Squeeze down on the bag during the soaking to help release the color. After soaking, bring the bath to the simmering point and simmer gently for 45 minutes. Remove the bag with the safflower and add enough water to the bath to make 1 quart of dye. For each ounce of wool to be dyed according to any of the following recipes, 1 quart of dye must be prepared.

### 71. Safflower with Alum (Yellow-Gold)

1 quart dyebath
2 skeins alum-mordanted wool (1/2 ounce each)

Place the 2 wet skeins of alum-mordanted yarn in 1 quart of dyebath and simmer gently for 45 minutes. Remove the skeins and rinse thoroughly. The yarn will be a rich yellow-gold color.

### 72. Safflower with Chrome (Gold)

1 quart dyebath
2 skeins chrome-mordanted wool (1/2 ounce each)

Place the 2 wet skeins of chrome-mordanted yarn in 1 quart of dyebath and simmer gently for 45 minutes. Remove the skeins and rinse thoroughly. The skeins will be a deep gold color, darker than the color from the previous recipe.

### 73. Safflower with Tin (Bright Gold)

1 quart dyebath
2 skeins unmordanted wool (1/2 ounce each)
1/16 teaspoon tin

Place the 2 wet skeins of unmordanted yarn in 1 quart of dyebath and simmer gently for 30 minutes. Remove the skeins and set them aside. Dissolve 1/16 teaspoon tin in 1/4 cup water and add this to the dyebath, stirring to assure even distribution. Replace the dyed skeins in the bath and simmer for an additional 15 minutes. Allow the yarn to cool in the dyebath and then rinse, first in soapy water and then in clear water. The skeins will be a bright gold color, brighter in intensity than the skeins mordanted with alum or chrome.

### 74. Safflower with Iron (Green-Gold)

1 quart dyebath

2 skeins unmordanted wool (1/2 ounce each)

1/16 teaspoon iron

Place the 2 wet skeins of unmordanted yarn in 1 quart of dyebath and simmer gently for 30 minutes. Remove the skeins and set them aside. Dissolve 1/16 teaspoon iron in 1/4 cup water and add this to the dyebath, stirring to assure even distribution. Replace the dyed skeins in the bath and simmer for an additional 15 minutes. Remove the skeins and rinse, first in soapy water and then in clear water. The yarn will be a green-gold color. If a deeper shade is desired, the skeins should cool in the bath before rinsing.

## Preparing the Dyebath for Yellow

1/2 ounce safflower petals

1 quart water

1 teaspoon baking soda

1/4 teaspoon citric acid

Dissolve 1 teaspoon baking soda in 1 quart of water. Tie 1/2 ounce safflower petals in a cheesecloth bag and soak this in the baking soda-water bath for 3 or 4 hours. Press down on the bag occasionally to help extract the color. The cheesecloth bag will soon become pink and then deepen to a crimson-red. After soaking, add 1/4 teaspoon citric acid to the dyebath. The addition of the citric acid will cause the bath to effervesce. Allow the bath to settle and it is ready to use. For each ounce of yarn to be dyed, 1 quart of dye must be prepared.

## 75. Safflower with Baking Soda and Citric Acid (Yellow)

1 quart dyebath

2 skeins unmordanted wool (1/2 ounce each)

Place the 2 wet skeins of unmordanted yarn in the dyebath and simmer gently at 150°F. for 45 minutes. Allow the skeins to cool in the bath. After cooling, rinse the skeins thoroughly. The yarn will be a light clear yellow. Alum-mordanted or chrome-mordanted skeins can be used instead to produce duller shades of yellow. Note that the cotton twine tied around the skeins has been dyed pink.

## 76. Safflower with Copper Sulfate (Light Green)

1 quart dyebath

2 skeins unmordanted wool (1/2 ounce each)

1/2 teaspoon copper sulfate

Place the 2 wet skeins of unmordanted yarn in 1 quart of dyebath. Warm the bath to 150°F. and simmer the yarn gently for 30 minutes. Dissolve 1/2 teaspoon copper sulfate in 1/4 cup water and add this to the dyebath, stirring to assure even distribution. Replace the dyed skeins in the bath and simmer for an additional 15 minutes. Allow the skeins to cool in the bath and then rinse thoroughly. The yarn will be a light yellow-green.

Note: The range of yellows and golds obtained with safflower offers a wide gradation of colors that can be especially effective when used for shading in a woven rug or tapestry.

# Camomile

## YELLOW-GOLD

Camomile (*Anthemis nobilis*), a perennial herb native to Europe, is of the same botanical family as golden marguerite (*Anthemis tinctoria*), sometimes called the dyers' camomile. Both have been used as a medicinal tea to calm upset stomachs, to soothe fretful babies, or even to aid sickly plants. The name camomile is derived from two Greek words: *chamai*, meaning "on the ground," and *málon*, meaning "apple." The camomile plant is used as a ground cover or between stones in a walking path and, when walked on, they produce an aroma (it may have resembled the smell of apples to someone long ago).

The plants have lacy foliage and grow to a height of ten to twelve inches. The color is contained in the flowers, stems, and leaves. The dried flowers may be purchased from dye supply houses, but it is also possible to find camomile tea bags at many gourmet shops. Either flowers or tea bags will work well. Another alternative is to grow your own camomile or golden marguerite plants.

### Preparing the Dyebath

1 ounce camomile flowers (or 6 tea bags)
1 quart water

Tie 1 ounce of camomile flowers or 6 tea bags in a cheesecloth bag and put this in 1 quart of water. Bring the bath to the boiling point and boil gently for 30 minutes. Remove the camomile and add enough water to the bath to make 1 quart of dye. For each ounce of yarn to be dyed according to any of the following recipes, 1 quart of dye must be prepared.

## 77. Camomile with Alum (Bright Yellow)

1 quart dyebath
2 skeins alum-mordanted wool (1/2 ounce each)

Place the 2 wet skeins of alum-mordanted yarn in 1 quart of dyebath and simmer gently for 30 minutes. Remove the skeins and rinse them thoroughly. The yarn will be a bright, clear yellow.

## 78. Camomile with Chrome (Gold)

1 quart dyebath
2 skeins chrome-mordanted wool (1/2 ounce each)

Place the 2 wet skeins of chrome-mordanted yarn in 1 quart of dyebath and simmer for 30 minutes. Remove the skeins and rinse them thoroughly. The yarn will be a rich gold color.

## 79. Camomile with Tin and Cream of Tartar (Orange-Yellow)

1 quart dyebath
2 skeins unmordanted wool (1/2 ounce each)
1/16 teaspoon tin
1/8 teaspoon cream of tartar

Place the 2 wet skeins of unmordanted yarn in 1 quart of dyebath and simmer for 30 minutes. Remove the skeins and set them aside. Dissolve 1/16 teaspoon tin and 1/8 teaspoon cream of tartar in 1/4 cup water and add this to the bath, stirring to distribute it evenly. Replace the skeins in the dyebath and simmer for an additional 15 minutes. Allow the skeins to cool in the dyebath and then rinse, first in soapy water and then in clear water. The skeins will be a bright orange-yellow.

## 80. Camomile with Iron (Olive Green)

1 quart dyebath
2 skeins unmordanted wool (1/2 ounce each)
1/16 teaspoon iron

Place the 2 wet skeins of unmordanted yarn in 1 quart of dyebath and simmer gently for 30 minutes. Remove the skeins and set them aside. Dissolve 1/16 teaspoon iron in 1/4 cup water and add this to the bath, stirring to distribute it evenly. Replace the dyed skeins and simmer for an additional 15 minutes. Allow the skeins to cool in the bath and then rinse, first in soapy water and then in clear water. The yarn will be a soft olive-green color.

## 81. Camomile with Copper Sulfate (Yellow-Green)

1 quart dyebath
2 skeins unmordanted wool (1/2 ounce each)
1/2 teaspoon copper sulfate

Place the 2 wet skeins of unmordanted yarn in 1 quart of dyebath and simmer for 30 minutes. Remove the skeins and set them aside. Dissolve 1/2 teaspoon copper sulfate in 1/4 cup water and add this to the bath, stirring to distribute it evenly. Replace the dyed skeins and simmer for an additional 15 minutes. Allow the skeins to cool in the dyebath and then rinse thoroughly. The skeins are a sharp yellow-green color.

Note: Other yellow flowers can be used as a substitute for camomile with much the same results. Goldenrod blossoms are rich in color and were used as a dye in colonial times, as were the flowers and stems of smartweed. Marigold flowers are also very rewarding as dye material. To obtain clear yellow colors, the yellow marigold blossoms should be used by themselves. A mixture of yellow and orange marigold blossoms will produce deep golds and oranges. These flowers may be used fresh or air-dried for future use, and they are prepared in the same manner as camomile.

# Black Walnut Leaves
## GOLD

The black walnut tree (*Juglans nigra*) has been used as a source of dye for many centuries. It was especially prized for the black and brown dyes produced from the hulls (see Recipes 99 – 105). Black walnut leaves are used both as a dye and as a type of medicinal tea.

Leaves should be gathered in the late spring when they are fully developed. They can be used immediately or air-dried for future use. For every ounce of yarn to be dyed, at least an ounce of leaves should be gathered. Be sure the leaves are thoroughly dry, then store them in a paper bag (moisture collects in plastic bags and could cause mold which would affect the colors produced). Black walnut leaves may also be purchased from dye supply houses.

Leaves from other trees—such as peach, birch, or poplar—and leaves from some bushes—the privet and mountain laurel for example—can be used in the same manner as black walnut leaves. They will produce various shades of yellow and gold depending on the mordants used.

### Preparing the Dyebath

1 ounce black walnut leaves
1 quart water

Place 1 ounce of black walnut leaves in a cheesecloth bag and add this to 1 quart of water. Boil gently for 30 minutes, pressing down on the cheesecloth bag to release as much color as possible. Remove the bag with the leaves and add enough water to the bath to make 1 quart of dye. For each ounce of yarn to be dyed according to any of the following recipes, 1 quart of dyebath must be prepared.

### 82. Black Walnut Leaves on Unmordanted Yarn (Yellow-Tan)

1 quart dyebath

2 skeins unmordanted wool (1/2 ounce each)

Place the 2 wet skeins of unmordanted yarn in 1 quart of dyebath and simmer gently for 30 minutes. Remove the yarn from the bath and rinse thoroughly. The yarn will be a tan color with overtones of yellow.

### 83. Black Walnut Leaves with Alum (Golden Yellow)

1 quart dyebath

2 skeins alum-mordanted wool (1/2 ounce each)

Place the 2 wet skeins of alum-mordanted yarn in the dyebath and simmer gently for 30 minutes. Remove the skeins and rinse them thoroughly. The skeins will be a rich golden yellow. The color may be deepened by allowing the skeins to cool in the dyebath before rinsing.

### 84. Black Walnut Leaves with Chrome (Gold)

1 quart dyebath

2 skeins chrome-mordanted wool (1/2 ounce each)

Place the 2 wet skeins of chrome-mordanted yarn in the dyebath and simmer, for 30 minutes. Remove the skeins and rinse thoroughly. The yarn will be a deep gold.

### 85. Black Walnut Leaves with Iron (Green)

1 quart dyebath

2 skeins unmordanted wool (1/2 ounce each)

1/16 teaspoon iron

Place the 2 wet skeins of unmordanted yarn in the dyebath and simmer gently for 30 minutes. Remove the skeins and set them aside. Dissolve 1/16 teaspoon iron in 1/4 cup water and add this to the dyebath, stirring to distribute it evenly. Replace the skeins in the bath and simmer for an additional 15 minutes. Allow the skeins to cool in the dyebath and then rinse, first in soapy water and then in clear water. The yarn will be an olive-green color.

## 86. Black Walnut Leaves with Alum plus Iron (Green)

1 quart dyebath
2 skeins alum-mordanted wool (1/2 ounce each)
1/16 teaspoon iron

Place the 2 wet skeins of alum-mordanted yarn in the 1 quart of dyebath and simmer gently for 30 minutes. Remove the skeins and set them aside. Dissolve 1/16 teaspoon iron in 1/4 cup of water and add this to the dyebath, stirring to distribute it evenly. Replace the dyed skeins in the bath and simmer for an additional 15 minutes. Remove the skeins and rinse, first in soapy water and then in clear water. The yarn will be a medium olive green with overtones of gold. The color may be deepened by allowing the skeins to cool in the dyebath before rinsing.

# Henna

## GOLD-ORANGE

Henna (*Lawsonia inermis*), a shrub native to Africa, Asia, and Australia, thrives in hot, dry climates. The ancient Egyptians used henna for dyeing their nails, the palms of their hands, and even the soles of their feet. Today henna is used in beauty parlors as a rinse that gives hair a reddish orange cast.

The coloring is contained in the leaves, which may be used fresh or dried. The leaves may also be powdered before using. Henna may be purchased from dye supply houses as dried leaves or as a powder.

### Preparing the Dyebath

1 ounce henna leaves

1 quart water

Break 1 ounce of henna leaves into small pieces and tie them in a small cheesecloth bag. Soak the henna overnight in 1 quart of water. The next day, bring the bath to the boiling point and simmer gently for one hour. Remove the henna from the bath and add enough water to make 1 quart of dye. For each ounce of yarn to be dyed, 1 quart of dye must be prepared.

### 87. Henna on Unmordanted Yarn (Yellow)

1 quart dyebath

2 skeins unmordanted wool (1/2 ounce each)

Place the 2 wet skeins of unmordanted yarn in 1 quart of dyebath and simmer gently for 45 minutes. Remove the skeins and rinse them thoroughly. The yarn will be a medium yellow color. If the skeins are allowed to cool in the dyebath before rinsing, a deeper color will be obtained.

## 88. Henna with Alum (Golden Yellow)

1 quart dyebath
2 skeins alum-mordanted wool (1/2 ounce each)

Place the 2 wet skeins of alum-mordanted yarn in 1 quart of dyebath and simmer gently for 45 minutes. Remove the skeins from the bath and rinse thoroughly. The yarn will be a golden yellow but deeper than the color achieved in Recipe 87.

## 89. Henna with Tin (Orange)

1 quart dyebath
2 skeins unmordanted wool (1/2 ounce each)
1/16 teaspoon tin

Place the 2 wet skeins of unmordanted yarn in 1 quart of dyebath and simmer for 30 minutes. Remove the skeins and set them aside. Dissolve 1/16 teaspoon tin in 1/4 cup water and add this to the dyebath, stirring to assure even distribution. Replace the dyed skeins in the bath and simmer an additional 15 minutes. Allow the skeins to cool in the dyebath and then rinse, first in a soapy water and then in clear water. The skeins will be orange in color.

Note: With any of the dyebaths, 1/16 teaspoon of iron could be added to sadden the color, or 1/2 teaspoon copper sulfate could be added to give a greenish cast.

# *Annatto*

## ORANGE

The annatto *(Bixa orellana)* is a small tropical tree native to Mexico and Central America. At the time of the Spanish explorations early in the sixteenth century, the Aztecs were using an annatto dye that they called "achiotl." From America its use gradually spread to Europe, Asia, and Africa.

The dyestuff is contained in the outer covering of the seeds of the annatto tree, and it is readily soluble in an alkali such as washing soda. An early book on basketry discussed annatto as a dye for rattan; today it is used not only as a dye for yarn, but also for butter, cheese, and varnish. Another use for annatto is to help "bloom" or give luster to yarn dyed with other materials.

### Preparing the Dyebath

1 ounce annatto seeds
1 quart water
1 tablespoon washing soda

Tie 1 ounce of annatto seeds in a small cheesecloth bag. Pound the bag with a hammer to break up the seeds, then soak it overnight in 1 quart of water. If a deep color is desired, add 1 tablespoon of washing soda to the bath. The next day, boil the bath for an hour, adding water if necessary as it evaporates. After boiling, remove the bag with the annatto seeds and add enough water to make

1 quart of dye. For each ounce of yarn to be dyed according to the following recipes, 1 quart of dye must be prepared.

### 90. Annatto with Alum (Orange)

1 quart dyebath
2 skeins alum-mordanted wool (1/2 ounce each)

Place the 2 wet skeins of alum-mordanted yarn in 1 quart of dyebath and simmer gently for 45 minutes. Remove the skeins and rinse them thoroughly. The yarn will be orange.

### 91. Annatto with Chrome (Gold)

1 quart dyebath
2 skeins chrome-mordanted wool (1/2 ounce each)

Place the 2 wet skeins of chrome-mordanted yarn in 1 quart of dyebath and simmer gently for 45 minutes. The skeins should then be rinsed thoroughly. The yarn will be a yellow-gold.

### 92. Annatto with Tin and Cream of Tartar (Bright Orange)

1 quart dyebath
2 skeins unmordanted wool (1/2 ounce each)
1/16 teaspoon tin
1/8 teaspoon cream of tartar

Place the 2 wet skeins of unmordanted yarn in 1 quart of dyebath and simmer for 30 minutes. Remove the skeins and set them aside. Dissolve 1/16 teaspoon tin and 1/8 teaspoon cream of tartar in 1/4 cup water and add this to the dyebath, stirring to distribute it evenly. Replace the skeins in the bath and simmer for an additional 15 minutes. Remove the skeins and rinse, first in soapy water and then in clear water. The skeins will be a bright orange, with greater intensity than the ones dyed in Recipe 90.

### 93. Annatto with Tannic Acid (Dull Orange)

1 quart dyebath
2 skeins unmordanted wool (1/2 ounce each)
1/2 teaspoon tannic acid

Place the 2 wet skeins of unmordanted yarn in 1 quart of dyebath and simmer gently for 30 minutes. Remove the skeins and set them aside. Dissolve 1/2 teaspoon tannic acid in 1/4 cup water and add this to the dyebath, stirring to distribute it evenly. Replace the skeins and simmer for an additional 15 minutes. Allow the skeins to cool in the dyebath and then rinse them thoroughly. The skeins will be orange, but have been darkened or dulled by the tannic acid.

# *Bloodroot*
## ORANGE

Bloodroot (*Sanguinaria canadensis*) is one of the first wildflowers to bloom in the spring in northeastern United States. Each plant produces a single white flower that stands above a large almost encircling green leaf. It grows in the shade and thrives on rich, leafy soil, sometimes reaching a height of ten inches. The roots or rhizomes are the source of the orange dye.

Bloodroot was an important dye material for the American Indians, who used it not only for dyeing cloth but also for coloring quills and rattles. Basketmakers, too, found it an agreeable dye for their wooden splits.

In many areas the bloodroot plant is on the conservation list and should not be gathered, however powdered bloodroot rhizomes are easily purchased from dye supply houses.

### Preparing the Dyebath

1/2 ounce powdered bloodroot

1 quart water

Tie 1/2 ounce of bloodroot in a small cheesecloth bag and soak it for several hours or overnight. After soaking, place the dyebath over low heat and bring it gradually to the simmering point (but not over 190°F. or it will dull the color). Simmer the bath for 20 minutes, or until the heating and simmering processes have taken a total of 45 minutes. Remove the cheesecloth bag and add enough water to make 1 quart of dye. For each ounce of yarn to be dyed according to any of the following recipes, 1 quart of dye must be prepared.

### 94. Bloodroot on Unmordanted Yarn (Orange)

1 quart dyebath
2 skeins unmordanted wool (1/2 ounce each)

Place the 2 wet skeins of unmordanted yarn in 1 quart of dyebath and bring it slowly to the simmering point. Simmer gently for 30 minutes. Remove the skeins and rinse them thoroughly. The yarn will be a golden orange color.

### 95. Bloodroot with Tin (Bright Orange)

1 quart dyebath
2 skeins unmordanted wool (1/2 ounce each)
1/16 teaspoon tin

Place the 2 wet skeins of unmordanted yarn in 1 quart of dyebath and bring it slowly to the simmering point over low heat. Simmer gently for 30 minutes. Remove the skeins and set them aside. Dissolve 1/16 teaspoon tin in 1/4 cup water and add this to the dyebath, stirring to distribute it evenly. Replace the dyed skeins and simmer for an additional 15 minutes. Remove the skeins and rinse, first in soapy water and then in clear water. The yarn will be a clear orange that is brighter than in the previous recipe.

### 96. Bloodroot with Alum (Red-Orange)

1 quart dyebath
2 skeins alum-mordanted wool (1/2 ounce each)

Place the 2 wet skeins of alum-mordanted yarn in 1 quart of dyebath and bring it slowly to the simmering point over low heat. Simmer gently for 30 minutes. Remove the skeins and rinse them thoroughly. The yarn will be a deep orange with red overtones.

### 97. Bloodroot with Alum plus Tin (Orange-Red)

1 quart dyebath
2 skeins alum-mordanted wool (1/2 ounce each)
1/16 teaspoon tin

Place the 2 wet skeins of alum-mordanted yarn in 1 quart of dyebath and bring it slowly to the simmering point over low heat. Simmer gently for 30 minutes. Remove the skeins and set them aside. Dissolve 1/16 teaspoon tin in 1/4 cup water and add this to the dyebath, stirring to distribute it evenly. Replace the dyed skeins and simmer for an additional 15 minutes. Remove the skeins and rinse, first in soapy water and then in clear water. The skeins have become a bright orange-red.

### 98. Bloodroot with Chrome (Warm Brown)

1 quart dyebath
2 skeins chrome-mordanted wool (1/2 ounce each)

Place the 2 wet skeins of chrome-mordanted yarn in 1 quart of dyebath and bring it slowly to the simmering point over low heat. Simmer gently for 30 minutes. Remove the skeins and rinse thoroughly. The skeins will be a medium brown with warm orange overtones.

# 5.
# Browns
# Blacks

# *Black Walnut Hulls*

## BROWN

The black walnut tree (*Juglans nigra*) has already been discussed as a source of gold dye made from its leaves (see Recipes 82 – 86). Its hulls have been used as a source of black and brown dye since antiquity. Gioanventura Rosetti, in his dyebook published in Venice in 1540, gives several recipes for different methods of using black walnut shells. One recipe tells how to combine the juice of the shells, furnace soot, and linseed oil to produce a solution to darken one's skin. He also furnished a recipe for a special bath water to use to remove the color.

A brown dye is extracted from the hulls of fresh walnuts. The color will be better if the nuts are gathered when they are fresh and green. They should be soaked for at least 24 hours (remove the hulls from the nuts first). The hulls are then boiled to extract the color. If the nuts are soaked for about a week, the boiling time for the hulls can be shortened. The hulls can also be air dried and stored for future use. Walnut hulls that are permitted to ferment will give an even stronger brown color.

The dye produced is color-fast even without a mordant, but additional shades of brown result from the use of various mordants. A black color can be achieved if used as an overdye with indigo or logwood. Walnut dye is also used as a saddening agent to darken other colors. Prolonged simmering of the yarn in the dyebath should be avoided as it tends to make the yarn harsh.

## Preparing the Dyebath

2 cups fresh black walnut hulls

1 quart water

Break 2 cups of walnut hulls into small pieces and cover them with 1 quart of water. If the pan is covered to keep the light out, the color produced will be darker. Soak the hulls for at least 24 hours (it is preferable to soak them for several days or a week to shorten the boiling time). After soaking, boil the hulls and water vigorously in the covered pan. If the hulls have soaked for a week, the boiling time is 60 minutes. With a 3 or 4 day soaking time, the boiling time would be 90 minutes; a 24 hour soaking should have 2 hours of boiling time to develop the full dye potential. It may be necessary to add a little water during the boiling. After boiling, strain the hulls from the dyebath and add enough water to make 1 quart of dye. This quart of bath can be used for any of the following recipes.

## 99. Fresh Walnut Hulls on Unmordanted Yarn (Tan)

1 quart dyebath

2 skeins unmordanted wool (1/2 ounce each)

Place the 2 wet skeins of unmordanted yarn in 1 quart of dyebath and heat until it is just warm to the touch (about 115°F.). Leave the skeins soaking in the dyebath overnight without additional heat. The next day remove the skeins and rinse thoroughly. The yarn will be a light tan color. The dyebath is by no means exhausted and could yield good color in any of the remaining recipes.

## 100. Fresh Walnut Hulls on Unmordanted Yarn (Brown)

1 quart dyebath

2 skeins unmordanted wool (1/2 ounce each)

Place the 2 wet skeins of unmordanted yarn in 1 quart of dyebath and heat the bath slightly (about 115°F.). Let the skeins soak for several hours or overnight without additional heat. After soaking, bring the dyebath and the yarn quickly to the simmering point. Simmer for 20 to 30 minutes depending upon how dark a brown is desired. Remember that a wet color is always darker than a dry one. When the yarn has reached the desired shade, remove the skeins and rinse thoroughly. After 30 minutes of simmering, the color is a warm brown. Interesting color gradations may be achieved by removing one skein after 20 minutes and the other after 30 minutes.

## 101. Fresh Walnut Hulls with Alum (Brown)

1 quart dyebath
2 skeins alum-mordanted wool (1/2 ounce each)

Place the 2 wet skeins of alum-mordanted yarn in 1 quart of dyebath and bring it quickly to the simmering point over high heat. Reduce the heat to low and simmer gently for 30 minutes. Remove the skeins and rinse thoroughly. The color is a richer and brighter brown because of the alum mordant. If a deeper shade is desired, the skeins may be left to cool in the dyebath overnight before rinsing. This procedure is preferable because a longer simmering time would make the yarn harsh.

## 102. Fresh Walnut Hulls with Iron (Dark Brown)

1 quart dyebath
2 skeins of unmordanted yarn (1/2 ounce each)
1/16 teaspoon iron

Place the 2 wet skeins of unmordanted yarn in 1 quart of dyebath. Warm the bath slightly (about 115°F.) and let the yarn soak overnight without additional heat. The next day remove the skeins and set them aside. Dissolve 1/16 teaspoon iron in 1/4 cup water and add this to the dyebath, stirring to distribute it evenly. Replace the skeins in the bath and bring it quickly to the simmering point over high heat. Reduce the heat to low and simmer gently for 30 minutes. Remove the skeins and rinse, first in soapy water and then in clear water. The skeins will be a dark brown color.

## 103. Fresh Walnut Hulls with Copper Sulfate (Greenish Brown)

1 quart dyebath
2 skeins unmordanted wool (1/2 ounce each)
1/2 teaspoon copper sulfate

Place the 2 wet skeins of unmordanted yarn in 1 quart of dyebath and bring it quickly to the simmering point over high heat. Reduce the heat and simmer for 30 minutes. Remove the skeins and set them aside. Dissolve 1/2 teaspoon copper sulfate in 1/4 cup water and add this to the dyebath, stirring to distribute it evenly. Replace the skeins and simmer for an additional 15 minutes. Remove the skeins and rinse thoroughly. The yarn will be a dark brown with green overtones.

## Preparing the Dyebath with Fermented Walnut Hulls

2 cups dried black walnut hulls

1 quart water

Break 2 cups of dried black walnut hulls into small pieces. Place them in a 2 quart pan or a large-mouthed plastic container and pour in 1 quart of water. Cover the pan or container and let it sit for 2 months or longer. During this time the mixture should be stirred about once a week. The walnut hulls will begin to ferment and decompose. Because a strong odor may develop, it is a good idea to keep the container in the basement or garage. At the end of 2 months the walnuts and water will have formed a thick brown ooze. Using fine cheesecloth, strain out the solid matter and add enough water to make a quart of dye.

## 104. Fermented Walnut Hulls on Unmordanted Yarn (Brown)

1 quart dyebath

2 skeins unmordanted wool (1/2 ounce each)

Place the 2 wet skeins of unmordanted yarn in 1 quart of dyebath and let them soak overnight. The next day bring the bath and yarn to the simmering point over high heat. Reduce the heat to low and simmer for 30 minutes. Remove the skeins and rinse them thoroughly. The yarn will be a warm medium-brown color. If the skeins are allowed to cool in the dyebath before they are rinsed, the color will be deeper.

## 105. Fermented Walnut Hulls with Iron (Dark Brown)

1 quart dyebath

2 skeins unmordanted wool (1/2 ounce each)

1/16 teaspoon iron

Place the 2 wet skeins of unmordanted yarn in 1 quart of dyebath and let it soak overnight. Although this soaking is not absolutely necessary, it will help deepen the color. The next day remove the skeins and set them aside. Dissolve 1/16 teaspoon iron in 1/4 cup water and add this to the dyebath, stirring to distribute it evenly. Replace the skeins in the bath and quickly bring it to the simmering point. Simmer gently for 30 minutes. Remove the skeins and rinse, first in a soapy water and then in clear water. The yarn will be a dark brown color.

# Cutch

## BROWN

Cutch, a dye made from the heartwood of the Acacia or Mimosa tree, was used in India long before the birth of Christ. The trees are native both to India and the East Indies.

To make the cutch extract, the trees are gathered when they are full of sap. The outer bark is removed, then the wood is cut into pieces and covered with water. This is boiled until much of the water has evaporated and the mixture becomes thick with the sap. It is allowed to cool and harden thoroughly, then it is cut into blocks.

Cutch when purchased from dye supply houses is a dark brown, almost black color. It is usually sold in small pieces that are shiny and look like little hunks of dark carmelized sugar. Cutch produces various shades of brown depending on the mordants used, and they all have a high degree of color-fastness.

### Preparing the Dyebath Solution

1/2 ounce cutch
1/4 teaspoon copper sulfate
1 cup water

Place 1/2 ounce cutch and 1/4 teaspoon copper sulfate in 1 cup of water. Boil the mixture, stirring it constantly. Cutch is extremely hard to dissolve and although the boiling is a slow process, it must be dissolved completely in order to obtain an even dye. Add more water as evaporation occurs to maintain one cup of solution. A fresh cupful of this solution is required for maximum color in each of the following recipes.

## 106. Cutch with Copper Sulfate (Brown)

1 cup cutch solution
1 quart water
2 skeins unmordanted wool (1/2 ounce each)

Place the 2 wet skeins of unmordanted yarn in 1 quart of water and bring it near the boiling point (about 190°F.). Remove the skeins and set them aside. Pour the quart of hot water into the cup of cutch-copper sulfate solution, stirring to distribute it evenly. Place the wet skeins in the dyebath and let them soak overnight. The next day remove the skeins, rinse, and allow them to dry. The yarn will be a medium brown.

## 107. Cutch with Copper Sulfate and Chrome Afterbath (Brown)

1 cup cutch solution
1 quart water
2 skeins unmordanted wool (1/2 ounce each)
1/16 teaspoon chrome
1 quart of water

Place the 2 wet skeins of unmordanted wool in 1 quart of water and bring it near the boiling point (about 190°F.). Remove the skeins and set them aside. Pour the hot water over the cup of copper sulfate-cutch solution, stirring to assure an even dyebath. Place the wet skeins in the dyebath and soak them overnight. The next day remove the skeins and squeeze out the excess moisture, but do not rinse. Dissolve 1/16 teaspoon chrome in 1/4 cup water. Add it to another quart of water and stir thoroughly. Place the wet skeins in the chrome bath and simmer gently for about 45 minutes. Remove the skeins and rinse them until the water is clear. The yarn will be a warm medium brown that has greater depth than the brown from Recipe 106.

## 108. Cutch with Copper Sulfate plus Iron (Dark Brown)

1 cup cutch solution
1 quart water

2 skeins unmordanted wool (1/2 ounce each)

1/16 teaspoon iron

Place the 2 wet skeins of unmordanted yarn in 1 quart of water and bring it near the boiling point (about 190°F.). Remove the skeins and set them aside. Pour the quart of hot water over the cutch-copper sulfate solution and stir thoroughly. Place the wet skeins in the dyebath and soak them overnight. The next day simmer the skeins in the dyebath for 30 minutes. Remove the skeins and set them aside. Dissolve 1/16 teaspoon iron in 1/4 cup water and add this to the dyebath, stirring to distribute it evenly. Place the skeins back in the dyebath and simmer for an additional 15 minutes. Remove the skeins and rinse, first in soapy water and then in clear water. The yarn will be a dark brown, but without the warmth of the color in Recipe 107.

Note: There is still dye potential left in each of these dyebaths. They may be used to dye additional skeins of yarn lighter shades of brown.

# Alder

## BROWN TO BLACK

Alder (*Alnus glutinosa*), also called black alder or European alder, was used in Europe during the fifteenth century as a black or brown dye. Gerald's 1639 *Herball* mentions poor country dyers using alder bark as a good black dye for their clothing, stockings, and caps. Indian tribes used alder bark as a dye for basket materials, and the Eskimos used it for dyeing reindeer skins.

The thick bark of the alder tree—dark brown on the outside and red-brown on the inner layer—is the source of the dye. The bark is very hard and should be broken into small pieces and soaked before using. A fifteenth century recipe used gallnuts to mordant the wool and then combined alder bark with green vitriol and gum arabic to make a black dye. Alder bark may be purchased from dye supply houses.

### Preparing the Dyebath

1 ounce alder bark
1 quart water

Chop 1 ounce of alder bark into small pieces. Tie them in a cheesecloth bag and soak in 1 quart of water for 3 or 4 days. After soaking, boil the water and alder bark for 2 hours. Keep the pan covered to reduce evaporation and add water if necessary during the boiling time. After 2 hours the bath will be a red-brown color. Remove the alder bark and add enough water to make 1 quart of dye. For each ounce of yarn to be dyed according to any of the following recipes, 1 quart of dye must be prepared.

### 109. Alder Bark on Unmordanted Yarn (Beige)

1 quart dyebath
2 skeins unmordanted wool (1/2 ounce each)

Place the 2 wet skeins of unmordanted yarn in 1 quart of dyebath. Simmer gently for 45 minutes and then allow the yarn to cool in the bath. Remove the skeins from the bath and rinse thoroughly. The yarn will be a warm beige.

### 110. Alder Bark with Alum (Tan)

1 quart dyebath
2 skeins alum-mordanted wool (1/2 ounce each)

Place the 2 wet skeins of alum-mordanted yarn in 1 quart of dyebath. Simmer gently for 45 minutes and then allow the yarn to cool in the dyebath. After cooling, remove the skeins and rinse them thoroughly. The yarn will be tan.

### 111. Alder Bark with Chrome (Golden Tan)

1 quart dyebath
2 skeins chrome-mordanted wool (1/2 ounce each)

Place the 2 wet skeins of chrome-mordanted yarn in 1 quart of dyebath. Simmer gently for 45 minutes and then allow the yarn to cool in the bath. After cooling, rinse thoroughly. The skeins will be a golden tan color.

### 112. Alder Bark with Copper Sulfate (Brown)

1 quart dyebath
2 skeins unmordanted wool (1/2 ounce each)
1/2 teaspoon copper sulfate

Place the 2 wet skeins of unmordanted yarn in 1 quart of dyebath and simmer for 30 minutes. Remove the skeins and set them aside. Dissolve 1/2 teaspoon copper sulfate in 1/4 cup water and add this to the dyebath, stirring to distribute it evenly. Replace the skeins in the bath and simmer for an additional 15 minutes. Allow the skeins to cool completely in the dyebath and then rinse thoroughly. The yarn will be a medium brown color.

## 113. Alder Bark with Alum plus Iron and Tannic Acid (Black)

1 quart dyebath

2 skeins alum-mordanted wool (1/2 ounce each)

1/16 teaspoon iron

1/2 teaspoon tannic acid

Place the 2 wet skeins of alum-mordanted yarn in 1 quart of dyebath and simmer gently for 30 minutes. Remove the skeins and set them aside. Dissolve 1/16 teaspoon iron and 1/2 teaspoon tannic acid in 1/4 cup water. Add this to the dyebath and simmer an additional 15 minutes. Allow the skeins to cool in the bath and then rinse thoroughly. The yarn will be a soft black color.

# 6.
# Overdyeing

# *Overdyeing*

The preceding chapters have dealt with one natural dye material at a time, with recipes developing the varied colors or gradations of color possible from that dye. With the use of different mordants you have seen how to go beyond the reds, yellows, and blues to oranges, greens, and purples—even to browns and blacks. This range of colors may be expanded even more by a process called overdyeing, or dyeing with one dyestuff and then modifying the color achieved by dyeing a second time with another natural dye material.

Overdyeing is not a new process. Some recipes for overdyeing are traditional, while others developed according to the individual dyer's whim. Yellows were very easy to achieve, and as long as one had indigo, greens were also possible. Red from madder overdyed with indigo could produce purples or deep dark blues depending on the strength of each dyebath. It is said that the reason the American flag is red, white, and blue is due to the fact that madder and indigo were reliable and fast dyes and naturally white yarn was always available.

## Procedure

The first step in overdyeing is to dye a skein according to a given recipe and then rinse it thoroughly. Be sure that all the excess dye is washed out or it will bleed into the bath used for overdyeing. (If care is taken to avoid bleeding, it will be possible to overdye several different colors with the same dyebath.) The rinsed, dyed skein is then placed into a second dyebath where the color undergoes a change. The yarn is left in the bath until the desired change has taken place and then it is thoroughly rinsed.

The following recipes for overdyeing are offered as suggestions for producing colors that will help fill out the possible color ranges for weaving or needlework projects:

## 114. Turmeric plus Indigo (Green)

Of all the colors produced with turmeric, Recipe 56 (Turmeric with Alum) produced the clearest yellow. Dye a skein according to Recipe 56. Rinse the skein until the water is clear and squeeze out all the excess moisture. Place the wet skein in a warm (130°F.) indigo dyebath (see p.63). Be sure to submerge it completely. Leave the skein in the bath for 5 minutes and then remove it, carefully squeezing out the excess dye. As the skein becomes exposed to the air, the indigo dye will begin to oxidize and the skein will become a medium green. Allow the skein to dry and then rinse it thoroughly. Repeated dippings and airings will deepen the color.

## 115. Turmeric plus Cochineal (Orange)

Dye a skein orange-yellow according to Recipe 58 (Turmeric with Tin). Rinse the skein until all the excess dye is removed. Then place the wet skein in a cochineal dyebath (see p. 43). Simmer the skein in the cochineal dyebath for 30 minutes. Remove the skein and rinse thoroughly. The yarn will be a bright orange.

## 116. Fustic with Madder (Orange)

Dye a skein bright yellow according to Recipe 48 (Fustic with Alum plus Tin). Rinse the skein until all the excess dye is removed. Place the wet skein in a madder dyebath (see p. 32) and simmer gently for 30 minutes. Remove the skein and rinse it thoroughly. The color of the skein will change from bright yellow to orange.

## 117. Barberry plus Indigo (Bright Green)

Dye a skein bright yellow according to Recipe 61 (Barberry on Unmordanted Yarn). Rinse the skein until all the excess dye is removed. Prepare a warm (130°F.) indigo dyebath (see p. 63) and completely submerge the skein in the bath. Leave the skein in the bath for 15 minutes and then remove it, carefully squeezing out the excess moisture. As the air causes the indigo dye to oxidize, the skein will become a sharp, bright green. Let the yarn dry, then rinse it thoroughly until the water is clear.

## 118. Madder plus Indigo (Purple)

Dye a skein of yarn red according to Recipe 5 (Madder with Alum). Rinse the skein until the water is clear. Prepare a warm (130°F.) indigo dyebath (see p. 63) and completely submerge the skein in the bath. Leave the skein in the bath for 15 minutes and then remove it, carefully squeezing out the excess dye (be careful not to agitate the indigo bath or bubbles of oxygen will be incorporated into the dyebath). Let the skein dry and then rinse it thoroughly. The yarn has changed from red to purple.

If madder skeins dyed a dull garnet according to Recipe 8 (Madder with Chrome plus Iron) are used with the indigo bath, the overdyeing will produce a dark navy blue.

## 119. Madder with Turmeric (Lustrous Red)

Dye a skein of yarn red according to Recipe 5 (Madder with Alum). Rinse the skein until all the excess dye is removed and the water is clear. Prepare a turmeric dyebath (see p. 74) and simmer the wet skein in the bath for 30 minutes. Remove the skein and rinse it thoroughly. The turmeric overdye serves to give added sheen or luster to the yarn without changing it to an orange color.

## 120. Fustic plus Indigo (Dark Green)

Dye a skein golden yellow according to Recipe 47 (Fustic with Alum). Rinse the skein thoroughly until the water is clear. Place the wet skein in a warm (130°F.) indigo dyebath (see p. 63), being sure to submerge the skein completely. Leave the skein in the bath for 15 minutes and then remove it carefully without agitating the bath too much. As the air causes the indigo dye to oxidize, the skein will become a dark green color. Allow the skein to dry completely and then rinse it thoroughly.

## 121. Black Walnut Leaves with Cutch (Dark Brown)

Dye a skein of yarn dark green according to Recipe 85 (Black Walnut Leaves with Iron). Rinse the skein until the water is clear. In a separate pan combine 1/4 ounce of cutch and 1 quart of water. Warm the bath over medium heat until the cutch is completely dissolved, stirring to keep the cutch crystals from sticking to the bottom of the pan. Place the wet skein in the cutch dyebath and simmer for 30 minutes. Remove the skein and rinse it completely. The yarn will be a dark brown.

### 122. Alder plus Cutch (Brown)

Dye a skein tan according to Recipe 110 (Alder Bark with Alum). Rinse the skein until the water is clear. In a separate pan combine 1/16 teaspoon iron, 1/4 ounce of cutch, and 1 quart of water. Warm the bath over medium heat until the iron and cutch are completely dissolved, stirring to keep the cutch crystals from sticking to the bottom of the pan. Place the alder-dyed skein in the iron-cutch bath and simmer for 30 minutes. Allow the skein to cool in the dyebath and then rinse it thoroughly. The yarn will be a rich brown.

### 123. Sandalwood plus Cutch (Rust)

Dye a skein red-orange according to Recipe 21 (Sandalwood with Alum). Rinse the skein until the water is clear. In a separate pan combine 1/4 ounce cutch and 1 quart of water. Warm the bath over medium heat until the cutch is completely dissolved, stirring to keep the cutch crystals from sticking to the pan. Place the wet skein in the warm cutch bath and simmer for 30 minutes. Remove the skein and rinse it thoroughly. The skein will deepen in color to a rust.

### 124. Black Walnut Hulls plus Indigo (Black)

Dye a skein dark brown according to Recipe 102 (Walnut Hulls with Iron). Rinse the skein until the water is clear. Place the wet skein in a warm (130°F.) indigo dyebath (see p. 63), being sure to submerge the skein completely. Leave the skein in the indigo bath for 15 minutes and then remove it carefully. The color of the skein will change from dark brown to black as the air causes the indigo dye to oxidize. After the skein dries, rinse it thoroughly.

### 125. Hemlock Bark plus Cutch (Orange-Brown)

Dye a skein rose-tan according to Recipe 13 (Hemlock Bark with Alum). Rinse the skein until the water is clear. In a separate pan combine 1/4 ounce cutch and 1 quart of water. Warm the bath over medium heat until the cutch is completely dissolved, stirring to keep the cutch crystals from sticking to the bottom of the pan. Place the wet hemlock-dyed skein in the cutch bath and simmer for 30 minutes. Remove the skein and rinse it thoroughly. The color of the yarn will be orange-brown.

These recipes for overdyeing are not meant to be a complete list of the possibilities. Experimentation will strengthen your knowledge of color and color mixing. Keep good notes as a guide for future overdyeing

One great application of overdyeing is to help salvage dyed skeins that seem too bland or different from the color desired. Save all such skeins to use in the following manner. Make a dyebath large enough and strong enough to accommodate all the skeins to be dyed (use 1 quart of dye per ounce of yarn). Place all the bland or off-color skeins in the dyebath and simmer for 30 minutes. Because of the range of mordants and the different dye materials used previously on the skeins, they will take on the new dye in different ways. They should be fairly harmonious, however, because of the common effects of the second dyebath. Some skeins may be simmered for a longer time if deeper shades of color are desired. Skeins dyed in this manner can now be used in projects where gradations or color shadings are needed.

# *Suppliers List*

With the growing interest in natural dyeing, new suppliers are continuously appearing in all parts of the country. To find a supplier near you, consult any recent issue of *Shuttle, Spindle, and Dyepot,* a quarterly magazine published by the Handweavers Guild of America, 1013 Farmington Avenue, West Hartford, Connecticut 06107. The following is a selection of suppliers that do a mail-order business.

Dyes and Mordants

Northwest Handcraft House Ltd.
110 West Esplanade
North Vancouver
British Columbia, Canada

World Wide Herbs
11 St. Catherine Street East
Montreal, Canada

| | |
|---|---|
| Dyes and Yarn | Dharma Trading Company<br>P.O. Box 1288<br>Berkeley<br>California 94701 |
| | Colonial Textiles<br>82 Plants Dam Road<br>East Lyme<br>Connecticut 06333 |
| | The Mannings<br>R.D. 2<br>East Berlin<br>Pennsylvania 17316 |
| Dyes and Fleece | Darrell Bailey<br>15 Dutton Street<br>Bankstown<br>New South Wales 2200<br>Australia |
| Natural Wool Yarn | Briggs & Little Woolen Mill Ltd.<br>Harvey Station<br>New Brunswick, Canada |
| | William Condon & Sons<br>65 Queen Street<br>Charlottetown, P.O. Box 129<br>Prince Edward Island, Canada |
| Yarn, Dyes, and Seeds | Straw Into Gold<br>5550 College Avenue<br>Oakland<br>California 94618 |
| Bulk Chemicals | Kem Chemical Company<br>545 South Fulton Street<br>Mount Vernon<br>New York 10550 |

# Bibliography

Adrosko, Rita J. *Natural Dyes in the United States*. Washington, D.C.: Smithsonian Institution Press, 1968.

Amsden, Charles Avery. *Navaho Weaving, Its Technique and History*. Glorieta, New Mexico: The Rio Grande Press, 1934.

Bemiss, Elijah. *The Dyer's Companion*. New London, Connecticut: Cady and Eells, 1806.

Berthollet, C.L., and A.B. *Elements of the Art of Dyeing*. 2nd. edition. London: Simkin and Marshall, 1824.

Bland, John. *The Forest of Lilliput, The Realm of Mosses and Lichens*. Englewood Cliffs, New Jersey: Prentice-Hall, 1971.

Bolton, Eileen. *Lichens for Vegetable Dyeing*. McMinnville, Oregon: Robin and Russ Handweavers, 1972.

Bronson, J. and R. *Weaving and Dyeing*. Boston, Massachusetts: Charles T. Branford Company, reprinted in 1949.

Bryan, Nonabah G. *Navaho Native Dyes,* compiled by Stella Young. Lawrence, Kansas: Haskell Institute, 1940.

Chamberlain, Marcia, and Candace Crockett. *Beyond Weaving*. New York: Watson-Guptill Publications, 1974.

Colton, Mary and Russell Ferrell. *Hopi Dyes*. Flagstaff, Arizona: Northland Press, 1965.

Cooper, Thomas. *A Practical Treatise on Dyeing and Callicoe Printing*. Philadelphia: William Fry, 1815.

Davidson, Mary Frances. *The Dye Pot*. Gatlinburg, Tennessee: M.F. Davidson, 1950.

Duncan, Molly. *Spin Your Own Wool and Dye It and Weave It*. Wellington, New Zealand: A.H. and A.W. Reed, 1968.

Feder, Norman. "Indian Vegetable Dyes, Part I and Part II." Leaflet 63 and Leaflet 71. Denver, Colorado: Denver Art Museum, Department of Indian Art, reprinted in 1969.

Fox, Helen Morgenthau. *Gardening with Herbs for Flavor and Fragrance*. New York: Dover Publications, 1970 reprint of work published by The Macmillan Co. in 1933.

Free, Montague. *All About the Perennial Garden*. Garden City, New York: The American Garden Guild and Doubleday and Co., 1955.

Gibson, Richard. *The American Dyer*. Philadelphia: Henry Carey Baird, 1872.

Goodrich, Frances Louisa. *Mountain Homespun*. New Haven, Connecticut: Yale University Press, 1931.

Hale, Mason E. *How to Know the Lichens*. Dubuque, Iowa: William C. Brown Co., 1969.

Hall, Eliza Calvert. *A Book of Handwoven Coverlets*. Rutland, Vermont and Tokyo, Japan: Charles E. Tuttle Co., 1966.

Harlow, William M. *Trees of the Eastern and Central United States and Canada*. New York: Dover Publications, 1957.

Hess, Katharine Paddock. *Textile Fibers and Their Use*. 5th. edition. New York: J.B. Lippincott, 1954.

James, George Wharton. *Indian Basketry and How to Make Baskets*. Glorieta, New Mexico: The Rio Grande Press, 1972.

Kierstad, Sallie Pease. *Natural Dyes*. Boston: Bruce Humphries, 1950.

Leggett, William F. *Ancient and Medieval Dyes*. Brooklyn, New York: Chemical Publishing Co., 1944.

Lesch, Alma. *Vegetable Dyeing*. New York: Watson-Guptill Publications, 1970.

Lloyd, Joyce. *Dyes from Plants of Australia and New Zealand*. Wellington, New Zealand: A.H. and A.W. Reed, 1971.

Loomis, Frederic B. *Field Book of Common Rocks and Minerals*. New York and London: G.P. Putnam's Sons, 1923. Revised edition, 1948.

Mairet, Ethel. *Vegetable Dyes*. New York: Chemical Publishing Co., 1939.

Martin, William, and John Child. *Lichens of New Zealand*. Wellington, New Zealand: A.H. and A.W. Reed, 1972.

Mason, Otis Tufton. *Aboriginal Indian Basketry*. Glorieta, New Mexico: The Rio Grande Press, 1902. 2nd. printing, 1972.

———. *Woman's Share in Primitive Culture*. New York: D. Appleton and Co., 1898.

Mellor, C. Michael. "Dyeing and Dyestuffs 1750-1914," *Color Engineering*. Sept.-Oct. 1968 and Nov.-Dec. 1968.

Milner, Ann. *Natural Wool Dyes and Recipes*. Dunedin, New Zealand: John McIndoe, 1971.

Partridge, William. *A Practical Treatise on Dying Woolen, Cotton, and Silk*. New York, 1834.

Rosetti, Gioanventura. *The Plictho*. Translated by Sidney M. Edelstein and Hector C. Borghetty. Cambridge, Massachusetts: The Massachusetts Institute of Technology Press, 1969.

Schetsky, Ethel Jane, editor. "Dye Plants and Dyeing-a Handbook," *Plants and Gardens*. Vol. 20, No. 3. Brooklyn, New York: Brooklyn Botanic Garden, 1964.

Stavrianos, L.S. *The World to 1500*. Englewood Cliffs, New Jersey: Prentice-Hall, 1970.

Taylor, Raymond L. *Plants of Colonial Days*. Williamsburg, Virginia: Dietz Press, 1952.

Thurston, Violetta. *The Use of Vegetable Dyes*. Leicester, England: Dryad Press, 1967.

Weigle, Palmy, editor. "Natural Plant Dyeing-a Handbook," *Plants and Gardens*. Vol. 29, No. 2. Brooklyn, New York: Brooklyn Botanic Garden, 1973.

White, Mary. *How to Make Baskets*. New York: Doubleday, Page and Co., 1902.

———. *More Baskets and How to Make Them*. New York: Doubleday, Page and Co., 1913.

Woodward, Marcus. *Leaves from Gerard's Herball*. New York: Dover Publications, 1969.

Zim, Herbert S., and Paul R. Shaffer. *Rocks and Minerals*. New York: Golden Press, 1957.

Zimmern, Natalie H. *Introduction to Peruvian Costume*. Brooklyn Institute of Arts and Sciences: John B. Watkins Company, 1949.

# Index

Alder bark: dyebath, 110-111; history and preparation, 110

Alder bark recipes: alum, 111; alum and iron and tannic acid, 112; chrome, 111; copper sulfate, 111-112; unmordanted yarn, 111

Alkanet: dyebath, 50-51; history and preparation, 50

Alkanet recipes: alum, 51; baking soda, 52; oxalic acid and cream of tartar, 51; vinegar, 51

Alum (as mordant), 14; recipe, 16

Ammonia (as mordant), 15

Annatto: dyebath, 95-96; history and preparation, 95

Annatto recipes: alum, 96; tannic acid, 96-97; tin and cream of tartar, 96

Baking soda (as mordant), 15

Barberry: dyebath, 77-78; history and preparation, 77

Barberry recipes: alum, 78; chrome, 78; iron, 79; tin, 78-79; unmordanted yarn, 78

Black (*recipes 45, 113, 124*), 60, 112, 118

Black walnut hulls: dyebath with fermented hulls, 106; dyebath with fresh hulls, 104; history and preparation, 103

Black walnut hull recipes: alum, 105, 106; copper sulfate, 105; iron, 105, 106; umordanted yarn, 105

Black walnut leaves: dyebath, 90; history and preparation, 90

Black walnut leaf recipes: alum, 91; alum and iron, 92; chrome, 91; iron, 91-92; unmordanted yarn, 91

# Notes

# Notes

# Notes

Edited by Jennifer Place
Designed by Bob Fillie
Set in 11 point Times Roman by Gerard Associates
Printed and bound by George Banta Company, Inc.

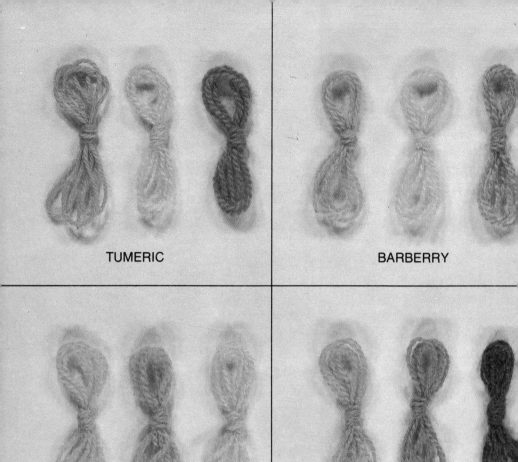

TUMERIC

BARBERRY

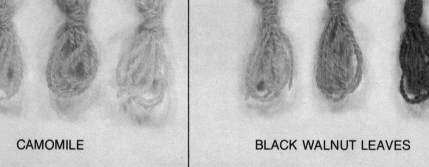

CAMOMILE

BLACK WALNUT LEAVES

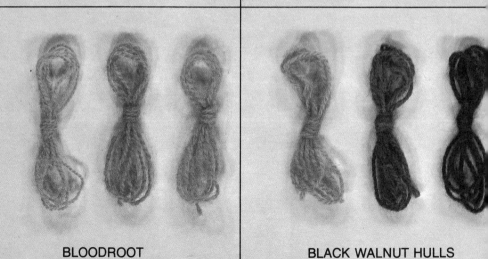

BLOODROOT

BLACK WALNUT HULLS